Beyond the Beginnings

BILINGUAL EDUCATION AND BILINGUALISM
Series Editors: Professor Colin Baker, *University of Wales, Bangor, Wales, Great Britain*
Professor Nancy H. Hornberger, *University of Pennsylvania, Philadelphia, USA*

Other Books in the Series
At War With Diversity: US Language Policy in an Age of Anxiety
   James Crawford
Bilingual Education and Social Change
   Rebecca Freeman
Continua of Biliteracy: An Ecological Framework for Educational Policy, Research, and Practice in Multilingual Settings
   Nancy H. Hornberger (ed.)
Cross-linguistic Influence in Third Language Acquisition
   J. Cenoz, B. Hufeisen and U. Jessner (eds)
Dual Language Education
   Kathryn J. Lindholm-Leary
Foundations of Bilingual Education and Bilingualism
   Colin Baker
Identity and the English Language Learner
   Elaine Mellen Day
An Introductory Reader to the Writings of Jim Cummins
   Colin Baker and Nancy Hornberger (eds)
Language and Literacy Teaching for Indigenous Education: A Bilingual Approach
   Norbert Francis and Jon Reyhner
Language Minority Students in the Mainstream Classroom (2nd Edition)
   Angela L. Carrasquillo and Vivian Rodriguez
Languages in America: A Pluralist View (2nd Edition)
   Susan J. Dicker
Language, Power and Pedagogy: Bilingual Children in the Crossfire
   Jim Cummins
Language Rights and the Law in the United States: Finding our Voices
   Sandra Del Valle
Language Socialization in Bilingual and Multilingual Societies
   Robert Bayley and Sandra R. Schecter (eds)
Learning English at School: Identity, Social Relations and Classroom Practice
   Kelleen Toohey
Learners' Experiences of Immersion Education: Case Studies of French and Chinese
   Michèle de Courcy
Multilingual Classroom Ecologies
   Angela Creese and Peter Martin (eds)
Negotiation of Identities in Multilingual Contexts
   Aneta Pavlenko and Adrian Blackledge (eds)
The Native Speaker: Myth and Reality
   Alan Davies
Power, Prestige and Bilingualism: International Perspectives on Elite Bilingual Education
   Anne-Marie de Mejía
The Sociopolitics of English Language Teaching
   Joan Kelly Hall and William G. Eggington (eds)
Teaching and Learning in Multicultural Schools
   Elizabeth Coelho
Trilingualism in Family, School and Community
   Charlotte Hoffmann and Jehannes Ytsma (eds)
World English: A Study of its Development
   Janina Brutt-Griffler

Please contact us for the latest book information:
Multilingual Matters, Frankfurt Lodge, Clevedon Hall,
Victoria Road, Clevedon, BS21 7HH, England
http://www.multilingual-matters.com

BILINGUAL EDUCATION AND BILINGUALISM 46
Series Editors: Colin Baker and Nancy H. Hornberger

Beyond the Beginnings

Literacy Interventions for Upper Elementary English Language Learners

Angela Carrasquillo, Stephen B. Kucer and Ruth Abrams

MULTILINGUAL MATTERS LTD
Clevedon • Buffalo • Toronto

Library of Congress Cataloging in Publication Data
Carrasquillo, Angela.
Beyond the Beginnings: Literacy Interventions for Upper Elementary English Language
Learners/Angela Carrasquillo, Stephen B. Kucer, and Ruth Abrams.
Bilingual Education and Bilingualism: 46.
Includes bibliographical references and index.
1. English language–Study and teaching (Elementary)–Foreign speakers. 2. Language arts
(Elementary) I. Kucer, Stephen B. II. Abrams, Ruth. III. Title. IV. Series.
PE1128.A2C348 2004
808'.0428'071–dc22   2003024122

British Library Cataloguing in Publication Data
A catalogue entry for this book is available from the British Library.

ISBN 1-85359-750-3 (hbk)
ISBN 1-85359-749-X (pbk)

Multilingual Matters Ltd
UK: Frankfurt Lodge, Clevedon Hall, Victoria Road, Clevedon BS21 7HH.
USA: UTP, 2250 Military Road, Tonawanda, NY 14150, USA.
Canada: UTP, 5201 Dufferin Street, North York, Ontario M3H 5T8, Canada.

Typeset by Wordworks Ltd.
Printed and bound in Great Britain by the Cromwell Press Ltd.

Contents

Acknowledgments

Many individuals have contributed to the development of this book. First, we are grateful to the English language learners we have had the privilege to meet as we visited and worked in classrooms. It has been the awareness of their needs and at times hidden strengths that has provided the impetus for undertaking this book. We also thank the many dedicated teachers who have shared with us their experiences working with English language learners. From these teachers we have gained a deeper understanding of the effectiveness of meaningful language and literacy activities. We acknowledge the graduate students in our classes whose ideas, questions, and experiences have helped shape the development of this book. Thanks are also due to Lourdes Willems who prepared the final format of the book. We thank the *Office of Research and Sponsored Programs* at Fordham University for the financial help for the last phase of this project. Finally, thanks go to Multilingual Matters, especially Tommi Grover and the editorial consultants Colin Baker and Nancy Hornberger, for their recommendations throughout the preparation of this book.

Angela Carrasquillo
Stephen B. Kucer
Ruth Abrams

Introduction

In recent years, there has been a great interest in the topic of English literacy development of English language learners (Freeman & Freeman, 2001; Hudelson, 1994; Schiffini, 1996). Educators around the world, and especially in the United States, are always in search of approaches, interventions, and instructional strategies to meet the language and literacy needs of learners whose languages and cultures are different from those of the school in which they are enrolled. More and more, educators realize that academic success and achievement do not depend on language proficiency alone, but also on students' literacy development and skills and knowledge of the various disciplines or content areas of the curriculum. As students progress through the grade levels, the demands of academically rigorous subject matter, combined with greater dependence on expository texts, make the attainment of academic literacy imperative (Schiffini, 1996).

A significant number of English language learners (ELLs) are unsuccessful in meeting grade-level academic demands. Through the years, this group of students often fails to attain grade-level literacy, and faces an increasing struggle to meet the academic demands of the curriculum. These students confront cognitively challenging content involving higher-order thinking skills such as analysis and evaluation. They need to develop high levels of literacy in order to achieve school language literacy demands, personal literacy goals, and societal expectations regarding the use of literacy skills in education, in work, and in other daily activities. Little research, however, has been conducted with second language learners who manifest difficulty in English literacy attainment in the upper elementary grades.

With the reauthorization of the Elementary and Secondary Education Act in 2001, and the creation of the *No Child Left Behind* legislation (US Department of Education, 2001), school districts across the nation must provide programs that are founded on scientifically-based research. School districts are hold accountable for meeting annual achievement objectives and measuring academic development. For ELL students, school districts must provide programs and activities with high academic standards that develop English proficiency, and must hold schools accountable for meeting annual measurable achievement objectives, including making adequate yearly progress.

Literacy acquisition and development is a cognitive process and the students' role is to actively and functionally use written language to construct meaning through a transaction with written text that has been created by symbols. As Hudelson (1994) explains, this mental transaction involves the reader in acting or interpreting the text, and the interpretation is influenced by the reader's past experience, language background, and cultural framework, and the reader's purpose for reading. Upper elementary students are supposed to read to construct meaning from their own texts and the texts of others, to learn about the world through the school curriculum, and to make and maintain connections with other individuals by identifying purpose in reading and writing. In addition to the above, English language learners (ELLs) need to acquire academic literacy in order to integrate themselves into the life of the school and the community at large. Literacy is also needed for academic success in school and ultimately for economic survival and well-being. In order to achieve, students require a classroom that provides an environment that is supportive of continuous language and literacy development. If students are going to succeed, schools must be prepared to make a long-term commitment to support the academic development of all students, including ELL students. Consequently, all teachers in all schools must address the learning needs of ELLs by individualizing their instruction to take into account the very different levels of English language proficiency and literacy development.

A major theme of this book is that the literacy gaps of struggling ELLs need immediate attention. If not, these gaps will increase as the demands of the curriculum increase. Because an increasing number of these 'struggling ELLs' appear in grades four to eight (Freeman & Freeman, 2002; Schiffini, 1996), this book addresses those English language learners who are enrolled in upper elementary grades between approximately grades four and six, who have fairly good knowledge of spoken English, and who are struggling with academic English literacy even though they have demonstrated basic English literacy skills. These children probably demonstrate phonemic awareness, knowledge of phonics, decoding, and word recognition. However, they demonstrate lower levels of literacy than would be expected of students in their age group and grade level. They have difficulties in producing the functions of literacy and using written language for communicating with others or for self expression. In general, these students come from two instructional or programmatic settings:

- ELLs who have left language assistance programs such as ESL and bilingual education without the appropriate English proficiency to tackle all instruction in English:
- ELLs who have been in English monolingual classrooms because their parents opt to enroll them in monolingual English classrooms, or because the school district does not offer language assistance programs.

There are terms that we use throughout the book and that we need to define in these introductory comments. One term used is that of the 'struggling English language learner' (ELL). English language learners is the label recently used among second language researchers and practitioners to identify students for whom English is a new or second language. We are encouraged to use the term throughout the book, and attempt not to use it to portray ELLs as deficient learners but as individuals who are learning through a second language. There is the need, however, to directly address the characteristics of this population: those who are struggling with the reading and writing demands of the curriculum. These students need strategies to ease them into trusting the functionality of reading and writing and to use literacy for purposes of communication and learning. Most struggling ELLs are in monolingual classrooms – classrooms where the teacher assumes that all children are proficient in the English language and are capable of meeting the high academic and linguistic demands of the curriculum.

Although the focus of this book is on how best to serve the literacy needs of struggling English language learners, this does not mean that we favor educational programs for ELLs that teach only through English. Nor does it mean that ELLs' culture and home language should be ignored by schools and replaced by English and the mainstream culture. On the other hand, this book puts the responsibility for educating ELLs in the hands of all educators, including those in English classrooms. These educators must use their professional competencies and resources in planning and delivering instruction to meet the literacy and academic need of ELLs. Planning and delivering instruction to meet the literacy gaps on the basis of ELLs' existing competencies, prior knowledge and experiences provides opportunities for helping these students to build and extend skills, knowledge and processes.

The highly complex process of language learning and literacy development calls for multifaceted instructional approaches. We propose strategies to help educators, especially teachers, to improve these students' English reading and writing. We have looked at the field of effective instruction, and in proposing strategies for struggling ELLs we have adapted many of the strategies found in the literature. The use of these strategies and suggestions would probably make schools more rewarding both for ELLs and for those who teach them. Strategies that we have modified include, among others, scaffolding, vocabulary development strategies such as rich semantic contexts, comprehension monitoring, comprehension strategies such as literature logs, instructional conversations to clarify and respond to text, narrative and expository writing strategies, sheltered instruction and problem-solving steps.

Organization of the Book

Much of the discussion in this book is based on the authors' interpretation of the research literature on children, on native English struggling readers, on second language learners' literacy development, and the recent evolving interest in ELL struggling readers, as well as our own research and observations of ELL classrooms. The book is divided in eight chapters:

Chapter 1, *English Language Learners*, describes the diversity of English language learners and provides an overview of the social, linguistic, cognitive and academic factors to be considered when identifying characteristics of those identified as 'struggling' in the mainstream classroom.

Chapter 2, *English Literacy Development and English Language Learners*, provides an overview of the nature of literacy and its development. It provides a conceptual framework for the instructionally-based chapters that follow.

Chapter 3, *Moving Beyond the Transition*, addresses the similarities and differences between monolingual and bilingual students and the unique literacy demands in the upper grades.

Chapter 4, *Instructional Writing Strategies*, presents various mediational structures and strategy lessons for promoting writing in the upper elementary grades.

Chapter 5, *Instructional Reading Strategies*, presents various mediational structures and strategy lessons for promoting reading in the upper elementary grades.

Chapter 6, *Language Across the Curriculum*, focuses on the identification of instructional strategies for teaching content area subjects to struggling ELLs so as to increase their content knowledge (concepts), vocabulary, and cognitive processes. A rationale for integrating language and content is provided, and suggestions are given for teaching ELLs in the content areas of social studies, science and mathematics.

Chapter 7, *A Framework for Assessment*, is divided in three main areas: (1) assessment of English language learners, (2) assessment of literacy for instructional purposes, and (3) assessment of literacy for accountability purposes.

Chapter 8, *Parents*, provides an overview of how educators can support parents in becoming collaborators with schools and how they support the academic development and advancement of ELLs who are struggling readers and writers.

CHAPTER 1

English Language Learners in United States' Schools

CHAPTER 1

English Language Learners in United States Schools

INTRODUCTION

As a result of shifting demographics, the United States has experienced increasing numbers of English language learners (ELLs) in its schools. This is due, for the most part, to the large wave of immigration and the high fertility rates among linguistically and culturally diverse groups in the United States. These new immigrants, refugees, international students, along with native-born non-English-speaking Americans, have a need to learn English and be successful members of the 'mainstream' American society. The passage of the 1967 Bilingual Education Act of the Elementary and Secondary Education Act (ESEA) and the landmark United States Supreme Court decision in *Lau v. Nichols* in 1974, provided a legal basis for equitable treatment of non-English-speaking students in United States during the last three decades (*Lau v. Nichols*, 1974). These two events impacted educational policy for non-English language communities and put linguistic minorities in the national spotlight, with the recognition that there is a large and growing number of students in United States schools who have little knowledge of the English language and need specialized language instruction. In 1968, the Bilingual Education Act provided funding to establish bilingual programs for students who did not speak English and who were economically poor. The 1974 Lau v. Nichols decision required every school district to take appropriate action to overcome language deficiencies in providing students equal participation in the instructional program. Today, there is recognition of English language learners/students (ELLs), and the many linguistic, academic and instructional challenges they face, and the need to provide these students with appropriate programs and effective instruction.

English language learners are found in every program and every school district, and they place great demands on teachers, administrators, and educational policy makers. Although many of them are initially placed in language assistance programs, a significant number of these students are enrolled in mainstream classrooms with no or little language assistance. The challenges presented to the schools by the influx of these students impact language specialists as well as regular/mainstream classroom educators. These students are not only required to compete with native speakers of English with respect to academic or literacy related language skills, they must also acquire the basic fluency in English that native speakers developed as a first language. Within such classrooms, students are expected to read longer literary texts, as well as texts in the content areas of mathematics, science, and social studies. In addition, English language learners need to develop the ability to understand native speakers of English in many situations, as well as the ability to read and write materials in English with comprehension and enjoyment. But the most crucial challenge for these students is the expectation of local, state, and national educational agencies that they score at grade level on state and national standardized tests, especially in the area of English language arts and mathematics.

These students are also expected to achieve a passing score in state content areas tests (e.g. New York State Regents exams). Therefore, educators need to find ways of meeting the needs of this significant group of students in achieving the English language arts standards as well as the content learning standards of the different academic subjects. The immediate academic achievement and future (employment) success of these students depends significantly on how successfully they acquire spoken and written English proficiency and develop strategies to appropriately use all the dimensions of the language. These dimensions include the specialized vocabulary of the various content areas, the ability to interpret and use complex syntax and grammatical structures in oral and written modes, and the use of reading and writing in all aspects of school life.

DIVERSITY WITHIN THE ENGLISH LANGUAGE LEARNERS' SCHOOL POPULATION

The English language learner population in the United States continues to be linguistically heterogeneous with over 100 distinct language groups identified (Carrasquillo & Rodriguez, 2002; GAO, 2001). Non-native English-speaking students in United States are foreign born as well as US-born. The US-born ELL students include speakers of American Indian languages as well as those children who were born and raised in non-English households. Children who are raised by parents who are not English proficient come to school with no or little knowledge of English. For example, Puerto Rican parents living in Philadelphia, who are first-generation monolingual Spanish speakers, converse with their babies using the language they have mastered, which in this case is Spanish. During their early years, these children are surrounded by their parents' language and culture, and in many instances their first encounter with literacy is in a language other than English. The Spanish language is the language of communication during the first four or five years. Relatives (adults and children) whose main tool of communication is in a language other than English surround the children with their language.

When the children go to church, the playground, the neighborhood store, all they hear is 'their language.' It is when they enter school for the first time that they are faced with an unfamiliar language (English). These children become 'double learners'; they begin to learn English as well as the grade level content curriculum. One group enrolls in language assistance programs such as Bilingual Education or English as a Second Language (ESL). Another group enrolls in all-English classrooms with a short period of English support services. For others, it is the 'swim or sink' approach of making them responsible and accountable for the learning of the language as well as for the content and skills of the curriculum. The extent of their integration in the society and their future employment depends significantly on how successfully they acquire English and use the English language for learning the demands of the school context and the demands of the English-speaking society.

On the other hand, the family of the foreign-born student may be voluntary immigrants or involuntary, uprooted refugees. These immigrants represent an important resource to the host country, a workforce whose services provide an important employment support in many communities. They may reside in the United States legally or as undocumented immigrants. Historically, immigrants have left their homelands to escape religious or political persecution, to flee from poverty and famine, or to seek land ownership or increased economic opportunity. Children of immigrant parents come from many different countries of origin, where curricular sequences, content objectives, and instructional methodologies may differ dramatically from American practices. Most of them enroll in American schools speaking only the language of their home or country of origin.

Whereas until the middle of the twentieth century the immigrants were predominantly from European countries, in the last four or five decades they have come predominately from Asian, African, Caribbean or Latin American countries. These immigrants are usually fleeing political and economical oppression.

Both groups (the US-born and the immigrant-born) are greatly diverse; they represent different ethnic and linguistic backgrounds, different schooling experiences and academic achievement, different lengths of time in US schools and different levels of native language and English proficiency. Most English language learners (about 66%) are enrolled in elementary schools, about 18% are enrolled in middle schools, and about 14% in high schools (GAO, 2001; US Department of Education, 1997; 2001). Although most of these students (almost 75%) speak Spanish at home, ELLs represent diverse ethnic backgrounds as well as diverse economic, experiential, educational and linguistic backgrounds.

THE 'TYPICAL' ELL STUDENT

The 'typical' English language learner student: (1) is characterized by a substantive participation in a non-English speaking social environment, (2) has acquired the normal communicative abilities of that social environment; and (3) is exposed to an English environment, most likely for the first time, during the formal schooling process. Upon entering school, English language learners may fall anywhere on a broad continuum of English language proficiency and English literacy development. The students may be entirely monolingual in the non-English language or may have some oral development in English with limited English academic language and literacy development. Their language and literacy vary and can have a significant role and impact on the way these students adjust and succeed in an all-English curriculum. For the most part, English language learners fall into three broad literacy groups relative to grade level literacy and cognitive demands. A brief description of these literacy groups follows.

ELLs Who are Literate in Their Native Language:
- demonstrate mastery of oral L1 vocabulary, oral fluency, grammatical and syntactical construction abilities;
- can read and write in the first language;
- demonstrate developmental and conceptual literacy;
- possess basic subject/content area concepts and functions;
- possess basic mathematical concepts and functions.

ELLs Who have Limited Literacy in Their Native Language:
- communicate in L1 with basic vocabulary, oral fluency, grammatical and syntactical construction abilities;
- have limited development of literacy and conceptual processes;
- may possess limited subject/content concepts and functions;
- may possess limited mathematical concepts and functions.

ELLs With Limited or Interrupted Formal Schooling:
- come from a country/home where a language other than English is spoken;
- usually enter a school in United States, after grade 2;
- upon school enrollment, have had at least two/three years less schooling than their peers;
- have limited native language literacy and poor academic achievement;
- usually have limited knowledge of science and social studies concepts;
- usually possess limited knowledge of mathematical concepts.

ELLs in All-English Classrooms

English language learners enrolled in all-English classrooms may come from two separate groups:

- Those students who may have exited from bilingual and ESL programs because they scored at the exit level in a standardized English proficiency exam. Usually, they demonstrate 'intermediate' to 'advanced' proficiency in English, as measured by a standardized proficiency test such as the BINAL, the LAB or the TERRANOVA.
- Those students who never participated in a language-assisted program and who receive all instruction in English. The English literacy skills of these

students vary depending on the level of proficiency in their native language, their length of English exposure, the quality of the instruction, and the English language support received.

These students are identified by the labels 'non-English speakers' 'limited English proficient' or 'English language learners.' However, the most recent label used in the literature is that of 'English language learners' (ELLs). The information gathered by identifying ELLs helps local educational agencies to request additional state or federal funding to provide appropriate instruction to these students. This information is also useful in determining the relationship between sources of funding and the nature of services provided. The United States federal government recommends that schools, at the beginning of each school year, begin the identification process by initially surveying and making a list of all students who meet one of the following conditions:

- the student was born outside the United States, or has a native language that is not English;
- the student comes from an environment where a language other than English is dominant;
- the student is an American Indian, or Alaskan Native and comes from an environment where a language other than English has had a significant impact on his/her level of English language proficiency; or
- the student has sufficient difficulty speaking, reading, writing or understanding the English language to deny him or her the opportunity to learn successfully in English-only classrooms, to be assigned to specific services, or to exit from the 'limited English' status, or services.

Although the data gathered are not always the most complete or accurate (i.e. some states or school districts do not always send the requested information or, if it is sent, it may be incomplete or inaccurate), these data provide information to researchers, policy makers and school personnel in making generalizations on the number of English language learners in the United States and the types of instructional services needed and provided.

Are All ELLs Identified?

Unfortunately, not all ELLs are identified. The identified English language learner population shifts from language assistance programs to all-English programs. Through scoring at certain expected cut-off scores in a standardized English proficiency test, English language learners exit from language assistance programs (usually ESL or bilingual education) and are then placed in 'regular' or 'mainstream' English-only programs. Once students are in this new placement, they do not qualify/count as designated 'English language learners.' A new group of immigrants or non-English-speaking United States children and youth arrive in the school district and are added to the number of English language learners who did not test out in the English language proficiency test.

Once those students are placed in mainstream classrooms, teachers plan and deliver instruction as if everyone in the classroom has reached the level of English-language proficiency that is needed to master the instructional content. Unfortunately, this instructional approach does not take into consideration that English language learners are cognitively taxed on two levels. On one level, they must learn the grade level subject content, and on the other level, they have the linguistic challenge involved in processing content and skills in a language (English) in which they are not yet fully proficient.

The types of instructional services provided by school districts to English language learners vary greatly and are dependent on several factors. These factors may be related to the size of the linguistically diverse population in the particular school or district, what resources are available locally, and whether the community/school district decides to provide native language content or English as a second language support to these students. In the United States, with the emphasis on learning/academic standards, and especially on meeting the English language arts curriculum standards, there is an emphasis in teaching English and through English to English language learners as fast as possible. And many English language learners do not receive any specialized language services, and are assigned to regular classrooms where they are mainstreamed with English-speaking students, in spite of their limitations in understanding instruction presented in English. Many of these students do not have the literacy skills of the different literacy demands of the curriculum. This means that regular classroom teachers who may or may not have the support of a language specialist, teach students who are English language learners. Consequently, the majority of English language learners receive most, if not all, of their instruction from classroom teachers, many of whom have had no specialized training in this area (Clegg, 1996; Fitzgerald, 1995). In many cases, teachers are not aware of English language learners' linguistic levels, cultural diversity, and their learning strengths and needs.

CHALLENGES OF ENGLISH LANGUAGE LEARNERS IN MEETING SCHOOL ACADEMIC STANDARDS

Providing instruction to English language learners needs careful planning, implementation of effective programs, a challenging curriculum, effective teaching and the provision of organized instructional and programmatic steps. However, authorities such as Cummins (2001), Krashen (1999) Thomas and Collier (1996; 1997) have cautioned that the choice of instructional programs for English language learners needs to be considered carefully, or these students will not succeed in the mainstream classroom. ELLs as well as educators are constantly challenged to meet the same academic standards as literate native English speakers.

The national educational initiatives envisage an educational system in the United States that holds all students to high common standards of world-class achievement. Learning standards represent a statement of the knowledge, skills and processes of what students can do over time as a consequence of instruction and experience. The idea behind the implementation of academic standards is that it will bring better teaching, more learning, and greater success for all students. Included in 'all students' are those identified and classified as limited English proficient/English language learners and all those not identified and who are enrolled in all-English classrooms with no or limited language assistance whatsoever. Our position is that English language learners may not have sufficient and adequate language and literacy functions or academic background to compete at grade level with native English peers. ELL students need mastery and systematic development of the following English literacy areas:

- a vocabulary for expressing themselves in different social and academic environments;
- automatic control and fluency in the use of natural and accurate English language, linguistic and grammatical patterns;
- natural communication situations for meaningful interaction;
- creative grammatical and syntactical construction abilities;
- development of strategies to confront the process and varied skills of reading;
- development of conceptual, grammatical and syntactical forms of writing.

LINGUISTIC AND ACADEMIC DEMANDS

Assessment data may not show ELLs' growth as they progress along the continuum toward mastering the curriculum and the academic standards as well as the English language and literacy functions. But, as students progress through the grades, the academic tasks they are required to complete and the linguistic contexts in which they must function become more and more complex and challenging. There are distinctive cognitive, language and literacy functions for the different subject areas. There are also general language functions applicable to most curriculum demands (e.g. seeking information, classifying, synthesizing, informing, hypothesizing, evaluating, analyzing, predicting, persuading, comparing). There are also academic 'registers' of schooling (features of speech, reading or writing tasks or activities of a particular discourse context or convention) that are challenging for English language learners. Salomon and Rhodes (1995) define these 'registers' as a variety of language, distinguished according to the use given. Students therefore, need to use particular styles of language to accomplish various academic tasks. These styles of language are associated with broad discourse levels of language. In other words, students are continually challenged by academic tasks requiring different and varied academic responses and different cognitive strategies. Salomon and Rhodes conclude that academic tasks influence the style of language to be used.

Cummins (2001), writing on these language and literacy functions (CALP: Cognitively Academic Language Proficiency), questions how prepared English language learners need to be so as not to rely on paralinguistic features such as body language, speech intonation, and sequence of events in order to understand language and comprehend meaning in meeting the demands of the different subject areas. ELLs need a strong language foundation, including basic vocabulary, knowledge of the academic world around them, and linguistic and cognitive ability to match with the instructional language and literacy demands and cognitive strategies of the grade level curriculum. The conceptualizations of Salomon and Rhodes (1995) and Cummins (2001) of academic language have made educators aware of ELL students' challenges in meeting the academic demands of the school curriculum. Figure 1.1 summarizes these challenges.

ELLs may have some of these skills in their native language that can ultimately be transferred to a second language; this transfer does not occur until a relatively high level of proficiency in the second language is acquired. English language learners need a level of reading and writing that enables them to function in an all-English school curriculum. While it is true that English language learners can greatly benefit

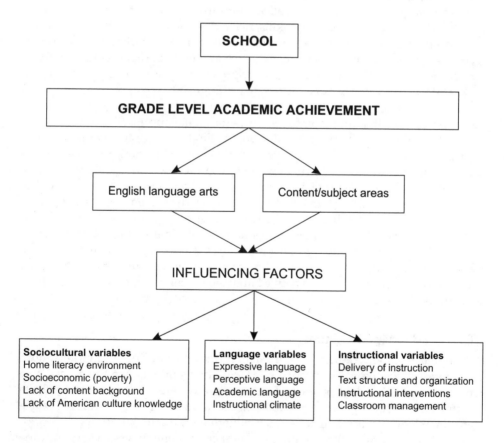

Figure 1.1 The academic challenges of English language learners

from the movement toward higher standards, all too often, this goal is frustrated by a myopic focus on English acquisition, to the virtual exclusion of other subject content. To break the self-perpetuating cycle of low expectations and academic failure, English language learners need to be given access to a challenging content, quality teaching and adequate educational resources appropriate to their grade level. To achieve the above objectives, ELLs need to enroll in high quality-programs (GAO, 2001) that include: (1) trained teachers, (2) clearly articulated goals, (3) appropriate and challenging curriculum and instruction, (4) systematic assessment, and (5) opportunities for children to practice their English.

LANGUAGE ASSISTANCE PROGRAMS

The most satisfactory instructional approach to meet the immediate needs of English language learners would be to place them in English language assistance programs. ELLs, whatever their school experience, their native language communicative and academic abilities, are called upon to advance simultaneously in the stages of developing interpersonal skills, mastering subject area content and skills, and acquiring academic language proficiency for each subject area – all in their second language. Two basic approaches are recommended to instruct students with limited-proficiency English skills. One approach uses exclusively English and makes little use of a student's native language (English-based approach/English as a Second Language), while the other makes much extensive use of the student's native language, often for a number of years (bilingual approach).

But the reality is that only a small group of English language learners receive instructional and language support through bilingual education, ESL, or compensatory education for basic instruction in English literacy and mathematics. As a result, there is no special provision for instructional and linguistic support for the many ELLs enrolled in mainstream classrooms to learn academic content and skills in English. A survey conducted by the United States Department of Education in 1997 indicated that, for those identified students with limited English proficiency, instruction was mostly through an English-based approach. About 85% of the schools enrolling identified ELLs offer ESL programs, and about 36% offer bilingual programs in which the student's native language is used to varying degrees. These two approaches are briefly summarized in the following paragraphs.

Bilingual Education Programs

The goal of bilingual education is to facilitate the education of children and youth by fostering a positive self-concept while facilitating students' cognitive, academic language expression. Instruction in English cognitive areas begins when students can function in that language and experience no academic handicap due to insufficient knowledge of the language. This bilingual instructional approach recommends that the school curriculum be taught in two languages, using both the students' native language and culture and English as a second language. In the

United States, bilingual education is an instructional tool to help students whose first language is not English to overcome their linguistic and academic difficulties and includes the expectation that ELL students will perform as well as their English-speaking peers in schools.

All bilingual programs include instruction in English as a Second Language (ESL) but some programs provide specialized instruction in English with native-language support for content area instruction. While non/limited English speakers learn English, they can also learn the content of the subject areas (social studies, science, and mathematics) in their respective languages.

The term 'bilingual education' covers a wide range of programs that vary from school to school and from district to district. The best known are 'transitional bilingual', 'maintenance/developmental bilingual,' and 'two-way' (also known as dual language) bilingual programs. *Transitional* bilingual programs emphasize the development of English-language skills in order to enable students whose proficiency in English is limited to shift to an all-English program of instruction. *Maintenance/developmental* bilingual programs provide instruction both in content areas and in language skills in the students' native language and in English. Instruction is designed to provide improved language skills in English as well as in the native language. In *two-way/dual-language* bilingual programs, classes include a mixture of native English-speaking students and native speakers of another language for instructional and social interaction purposes. The English speakers learn a second language at the same time as the non-English speakers learn English. A major strength of the two-way/dual-language bilingual program is that the two groups of students act as linguistic models for one another.

English as Second Language Programs

English as a Second Language (ESL) is the recommended instructional approach when there are many language groups represented in one classroom, or when bilingual education is not feasible or desired in a school district. It is designed to meet the immediate communication and literacy needs of students whose proficiency in English is limited or non-existent by providing them with the language skills they need to communicate with teachers and peers and to receive content matter in English. ESL is designed to complement the practice and exposure to English that students receive inside and outside the scheduled English classes. ESL classes provide students with instruction at their level of English proficiency. Appropriate ESL programs practice the following principles:

(1) emphasize communication and meaning;
(2) integrate the four areas of functional contexts of learning and communication development: listening, speaking, reading and writing,;
(3) recognize students prior linguistic conceptual and cultural experiences to build proficiency in English;
(4) respect the values and traditions of students' cultural heritage;

(5)   provide for the continuation of conceptual development, learning and communication.

Although there is a diversity of ESL programs, the most popular in the United States is the pull-out program in which instruction is based on a special curriculum taught in English, and is offered during specific school periods. The students' program of pull-out ESL is easy to schedule and it is financially feasible for school districts. Students are usually 'pulled-out' of the classroom to receive language assistance by a specialized second language teacher.

A recent popular language assistance approach is 'sheltered English,' which emphasizes simplified vocabulary, grammar and sentence structure in teaching English through the content areas (Echeverria & Graves, 1999). In this model, every lesson in every subject area becomes, in part, a language lesson. Vocabulary and language skills are taught in tandem with relevant concepts.

Sources of Funding for English Language Development Programs for ELLs

Although educating students is primarily a state and local responsibility, the federal government has a substantial role in ensuring that the educational needs of students with limited English proficiency (LEP) are met. This role is based on Title VI of the Civil Rights Act of 1964 and court decisions interpreting the instructional equal rights of ELL/LEPs. In 2001, the United States Congress, in approving the Elementary and Secondary Education Act (ESEA)/*No Child Left Behind,* changed the name of the office in charge of providing appropriate instructional programs for ELLs to learn English and attain high levels of content area achieved from the Office of Bilingual Education and Minority Language Affairs to the Office of English Language Acquisition and Language Enhancement. This recent federal law is known as Title III: English Language Acquisition, Language Enhancement, and Academic Achievement Act. States receive funds to distribute among school districts based on the number of English language learners in their respective school districts.

'STRUGGLING' ENGLISH LANGUAGE LEARNERS

Our classroom observations of struggling ELLs, and those of our graduate students, have helped us to make several observations on struggling ELL readers and writers. These generalizations are in no way a typical profile of these students; they provide a checklist of behaviors/indicators to be referred to when teaching English literacy. The 'struggling' ELL population faces unique and diverse challenges, and their linguistic and cognitive 'struggles' vary from student to student depending on many factors such as years in the United States, experiences in the formal learning of English, language assistance received, cognitive and learning abilities, level of English language proficiency, and the academic demands of the school curriculum (especially those of the different subject areas). In general, these students are below grade level in reading, writing, and mathematics, have not mastered the cognitive and linguistic strategies to construct meaning from text, and do not appropriately communicate to different audiences in writing. In the 1980s, Oller and Perkins' research suggested that different language skills do tend to correlate moderately well, and if a variety of measures of speaking, reading or writing are analyzed, a global underlying language dimension is identified which they called a 'global language proficiency' (Oller & Perkins, 1989). And although we do not agree with the totality of this theory, we see a relationship between students' overall level of cognitive development, their mastery of the first language, if any, and their predisposition to learn the English language. Consequently, since most literacy skills are transferable among languages, ELL students with mastery of native language literacy skills may transfer these skills into their second language. We hypothesize that this is perhaps not the case with the 'struggling ELL,' and that the low English literacy of a significant group of ELLs stems from their difficulty in developing a cognitive language framework or foundation for learning English and English literacy (reading and writing). These students may not have the required language (in L1 or L2) to cope with grade-level school curriculum skills and testing demands.

In addressing 'struggling English language learners,' perhaps the best way of depicting their diversity is to describe typical students who may be found in most large public school districts in the nation. The four students described below are representative of ELL struggling readers and writers and, although they do not represent every struggling English language learner, their academic profile provides linguistic, cognitive, and academic characteristics that are useful in describing ELL individuals of low English literacy.

Wang

Wang is a fifth grader who came to the United States from Hong Kong five years ago. He attended a bilingual Kindergarten class for six months and, because his parents want him to succeed in America, he was placed in an all-English kindergarten classroom, with one period of ESL instruction per day. However, his parents were not happy with their son's academic development and level of English proficiency, and transferred him to another neighborhood school.

Although Wang is very attentive in class and tries to complete all academic tasks assigned in class, he finds that he does not have the speed or 'talent' of other students in the class. Although he tries to concentrate during silent reading, he does not understand many of the words and sentences in the short stories he reads. He finds that, although he is interested in certain topics, he is very easily distracted and quickly loses the meaning or plot of the story. In addition, he has difficulties in following directions even when they are given in a step-by-step format. For a fifth grade student, Wang's social language and vocabulary are limited. His English literacy is still emerging and he has not yet reached the point where he is able to read and understand the information in the science and social studies textbooks.

Mirqueya

Mirqueya moved to New York City from the Dominican Republic at the age of six and a half. Although Mirqueya came from a two-parent household, when she moved to the United States, she was accompanied only by her mother. Spanish was and continues to be the only language spoken at home. At the recommendation of the assistant principal, Mirqueya was placed in a monolingual English-speaking second grade class (with 45 minutes of daily ESL instruction). During her second and third grades, Mirqueya was frequently absent from school from one to two weeks. The reason for the absences was that she had to go to the Dominican Republic to visit her father.

Mirqueya is now in fourth grade. Several months have passed, and she does not participate in class discussions and does not engage, or finish reading and writing tasks. Her homework is either incorrectly done or not done at all. During playtime, Mirqueya prefers to play with other Dominican children from other classes. She receives one hour of ESL pull-out assistance, usually when her classmates are engaged in English language arts. While attending ESL instruction, she receives intensive oral language development, with vocabulary enrichment as well as listening comprehension development. Because Mirqueya has been in the US for about three years, she is scheduled to take the standardized English language arts test this spring. When the teacher informs Mirqueya's mother of the spring testing challenge, her mother's response is, 'Oh, she will pass, because she speaks very good English.'

Sasha

Sasha is a sixth-grade student in a suburban school district. She and her sister were adopted from a Russian orphanage by a US couple six years ago. Neither of her adoptive parents speak the Russian language. When Sasha arrived from Russia, their US parents invited friends who spoke Russian to engage in conversations and games with Sasha and her sister to make their language and cultural transition a little easier.

At the present time, Sasha's level of conversational English is satisfactory for her age and years in the US. However, she is at the beginning level of academic English proficiency, performing at a second-grade level in literacy activities. Sasha can recognize high-frequency words and uses the reading strategy of sounding out words to decode then but when she is asked to give an oral retelling of the story, she can name primary characters but cannot identify the setting or the plot of the story. Although Sasha is able to decode most of the English words, she does not comprehend what she reads, especially in the social studies or science textbooks. Last year, she scored at a second grade level in the English language arts standardized exam. She is afraid that she will also score low in the standardized mathematics test she needs to take this year.

Karl

Karl is an 11-year-old boy of Haitian descent who entered 6th grade at a local public middle school. He was born in the United States, the oldest of three children. Karl's parents were born in Haiti and came to New York 15 years ago to improve their economic situation. They both work, and Karl's grandmother looks after the children and helps out with the cooking and cleaning. Karl's family interacts mainly with Haitian friends. Karl's parents have no time to go to school to check on their children, but as the children have never had to repeat a grade, they think everything is going satisfactorily in school. Before Karl started 6th grade, the family moved twice because of loss of employment for one or both parents. Karl and several friends have formed a rap group, and he is a member of the Haitian Little League Club. He likes to talk with his 6th grade teacher and classmates, and told his teacher that he never reads or writes at home, although he sometimes writes words for songs with his friends' rap group. Karl confessed that, although he speaks English well, English is his primary language, and he speaks English all the time, he is afraid of participating in class discussions. He says that most of the time, at the silent reading time, he pretends that he is reading but in reality he is 'day dreaming' about baseball or the rap band. He also told the teacher that reading and writing are 'boring.' Karl's dislike of reading has contributed to his lack of interest in mathematics, science and social studies classes. However, because he likes to talk, he thinks of himself as a 'very smart individual.'

Wang, Mirqueya, Sasha and Karl: English Literacy Gaps

Examining the English literacy characteristics of Wang, Mirqueya, Sasha and Karl is helpful in identifying indicators, behaviors and possible factors contributing to the achievement gap between struggling ELLs and the rest of the school population. These students are representative of two groups: (1) those born outside the US who are placed in English-only classrooms without the necessary English proficiency and (2) those born in the US who have not developed enough academic language to succeed at grade level curriculum. The first group faces the complex task of advancing in conversational English, becoming literate in English, and gaining the academic knowledge and skills needed to compete academically with native speakers of English. Many of the students do not have sufficient literacy background even in their first language; they often struggle with course work, and do not score well on standardized tests. The second group appears to be English proficient, but the students have been unable to continue developing their English literacy at the level required by the school curriculum and the learning standards. The reasons, perhaps, are that they may not have received constant support programs, and may have missed school for extended periods of time. Most of these students demonstrate conversational English fluency, but lack the academic language proficiency they need to survive in school. The consequences of a slow

Table 1.1 ELLs' achievement and English language literacy gaps

Indicators	Possible factors
Below (at least two years) in reading and writing.	Gaps in formal schooling accompanied by transition to English as a new language.
May have adequate grades, but score low on tests;.	Inadequate preschool experiences.
Lack basic concepts in the different subject/content areas.	Families live in poverty, and experience tragedies and extreme hardships.
Limited English proficiency.	They move often as parents seek better financial/economical opportunities.
Lack the general language comprehension ability to accurately and fluently identify and interpret printed material.	Level of academic language proficiency not sufficient for them to survive in all-English classrooms.
Lack of knowledge and active application of specific reading strategies.	Have had no consistent school program.
Academic achievement and limited language proficiencies get cumulatively worse over time, over grade levels, and across all subject areas.	
Limited expressive and receptive vocabulary.	
Consciously think about language production and are stilted and uncreative with language.	
Mismatch between student's perception of achievement and actual grade or test scores.	
Find it difficult to think and to orally express himself/herself.	

start in reading and writing become monumental as they accumulate exponentially over time. Table 1.1 summarizes the challenges these students face, and the possible causes.

Are these students struggling in all language abilities? Do students who perform poorly on spelling tests also perform poorly in oral comprehension tests? Rather than highlighting the 'apparent' deficit of these students, the more positive approach is to emphasize that, when suitable conditions are provided, ELLs are capable of achieving high levels of English literacy. Educators need to locate the causes of the deficit (e.g. quality of instruction, lack of early literacy development) and implement instructional interventions and strategies to move students up the ladder of literacy development. These interventions need to occur as early as possible, because children who get off to a poor start in reading rarely catch up.

CONCLUSION

Major shifts in political and economic systems on a global scale have resulted in demographic changes worldwide. Industrialized nations have experienced great influxes of immigrants from poorer, less-developed countries. The rise in ethnic and civil strife has also affected the rate of immigration in various parts of the world. As in other parts of the world, the impact of these demographic changes has also been experienced in the United States. The arrival of new immigrants to the United States has brought about increased linguistic as well as cultural diversity, and has altered the ethnic composition of the general population. The rapid escalation of culturally and linguistically diverse groups is most apparent among the nation's young and school-aged population. Such a trend in linguistic and cultural diversification can create new opportunities for the nation. Many individuals in this rapidly increasing population constitute a growing proportion of the nation's future workforce. The asset of proficiency in more than one language that a linguistically-diverse population offers increases in value as the world moves toward an interdependent global economy. At the same time, this diversification presents new challenges for educators and schools, as attention has become increasingly focused on improving the language learning of ELLs, particularly in the area of literacy.

ELLs, like their monolingual counterparts, need to know not only the processes of reading and writing, but also how to use reading and writing to learn. Our challenge as educators is to provide educational contexts that will both support these students' English language development, while at the same time tap into the linguistic resources offered by their knowledge of another language. To do this and be effective teachers of literacy requires that we have theoretically-based knowledge of how literacy learning occurs and that our instructional approaches are research-based (Tompkins, 2001). As educators, we face the challenge of making ELLs successful learners and successful students.

CHAPTER 2

English Literacy Development and English Language Learners: A Theoretical Overview

CHAPTER 2

English Literacy Development and English Language Learners: A Theoretical Overview

INTRODUCTION

As was discussed in Chapter 1, the increasing number of school-aged children who are entering our school systems from households where the home language is one other than English presents us as educators with opportunities and challenges. We can appreciate the opportunities offered to us as a nation when we consider the asset that proficiency in more than one language offers to our workforce as we move into an increasingly global economy. The challenges are apparent as we consider that language is the primary vehicle of instruction in our schools, yet often these students have difficulty benefiting from that instruction because of their limited proficiency in English, the language of the classroom (De Avila, 1997). To address this latter consideration and to enable us to provide optimal opportunities for English language learners (ELLs) to achieve academic success, it is essential that we examine our existing pool of language and literacy knowledge as it pertains to bilingual language users. To do this, we need to ground our view of literacy in a theoretical framework that includes an understanding of literacy in a second language and second language proficiency.

Although, as bilingual language users, ELLs bring a unique reservoir of resources to the literacy task, as they read and write they engage in basically the same processes and strategies as those used by their monolingual counterparts (Jimenez, 1992; Kucer, 2001). For this reason, and also because theoretical models of second language literacy are currently evolving, in the discussion presented in this chapter, we rely on first language (L1) frameworks of literacy to guide our understanding of second language (L2) literacy development.

It is imperative for educators planning for the academic development of ELLs to have an understanding of how an individual learns a second language. A key question is, 'What level of second language proficiency is necessary for an individual to use that language as a vehicle for learning academic content?' In this chapter, we will address that question as we discuss the theoretical position that makes a fundamental distinction between the conversational and the academic aspects of language proficiency. The implications of this distinction are that, in planning instructional experiences for ELLs, we need to ensure that students are challenged cognitively and at the same time receive the linguistic and contextual scaffolding that will enable them to complete academic tasks successfully (Cummins, 2001)

To help us understand the conceptual basis for the instructional strategies discussed in later chapters, the first section of this chapter provides us with an overview of first language literacy and its development. The second section presents information that relates to second language acquisition. In the final section, we focus on some of the unique issues involved in planning ELLs' English literacy instruction.

THE NATURE OF FIRST LANGUAGE LITERACY AND ITS DEVELOPMENT

In this section, we present our view of literacy learning and the theoretical bases from which it emerges. We refer to particular L1 literacy models and theories that we believe support an understanding of L2 reading and writing. This is necessary because theoretical models of L2 literacy are still at the exploratory stage.

Our view of literacy and how children learn to read and write comes out of a constructivist understanding in which readers and writers are engaged in making meaning from and with text (oral and written language). In a constructivist classroom, children are active learners and are encouraged to be linguistic and cognitive explorers, making connections between new information and their prior knowledge. Teachers act as facilitators who mediate children's learning, rather than as transmitters of information. Support for the constructivist view can be found in three perspectives that have influenced our understanding of literacy over the past four decades. These are: the psycholinguistic perspective, the cognitive-interactive perspective, and the sociocultural perspective. Understanding gleaned from each of these perspectives enables us to conceptualize the literacy process as comprised of multiple dimensions (Kucer, 2001; Ruddell *et al.*, 1994).

The Psycholinguistic Dimension of Literacy

Psycholinguists view readers and writers as language users who make use of language cues as they engage in literacy tasks (Goodman, 1967). In reading, the reader makes use of syntactic, semantic, and graphophonemic cueing systems to make meaning from the text:

- *Syntactic cues:* the word order provides grammatical information that allows the reader to predict what type of word (e.g. noun) will come next in the sentence.

- *Semantic cues:*the reader use knowledge of word meaning to predict the word (e.g. a house is a structure in which people live).
- *Graphophonemic cues:*the reader uses knowledge of letter-sound relationships to predict what the word might possibly be (e.g. in English, the 'ph' often makes an 'f' sound).

Psycholinguists have also given us a means for understanding how a reader is processing the text and constructing meaning through miscue analysis (Goodman *et al.*, 1987). What previously had been considered errors or mistakes are understood to be 'miscues.' Rather than consider these miscues as negative occurrences that need to be eliminated, miscues are viewed as opportunities that provide a window into the inner workings of the reader's comprehension processes. All readers make miscues; good readers, however, make miscues that preserve the meaning of the text, whereas struggling readers make miscues that disrupt meaning (see Chapter 7).

In the psycholinguistic perspective, literacy is considered to be a constructive process in which individuals are able to make sense of new information by relating it to what they already know (Smith, 1971). Consequently, the primary focus of literacy instructional activities and experiences is on making meaning, and the language of the materials used should reflect natural linguistic patterns.

The Cognitive-Interactive Dimension of Literacy

The explorations of the cognitive psychologists have provided us with a 'window' into mental processes that readers and writers engage in as they construct meaning through written language. Among the insights into literacy processing that have occurred as a result of this research, we have gained a fuller understanding of the prominent role played by the individual's background knowledge in meaning making from and with text.

As readers interact with text, they make use of their background knowledge, or what has been called 'schema' (Rumelhart, 1980; Spiro *et al.*, 1987). According to schema theory, prior knowledge is stored in structures or schemata, which are like files in the mind. When an individual encounters new information, these 'files' are reorganized. Readers draw on their prior knowledge (reader-based information) and information found in the text (text-based information) to construct meaning. Readers make use of both top-down processing (e.g. use of their prior knowledge, reading expectations) and bottom-up processing (e.g. semantics, syntax, graphophonemics). Readers draw on their word-identification skills (bottom-up) and comprehension strategies (top-down) as they read. As word-identification skills develop and as readers gain fluency, meaning making is enhanced.

The Sociocultural Dimension of Literacy

Sociolinguists have expanded our understanding of literacy by demonstrating the social and cultural dimensions of reading and writing. There is an interrelationship between thought and language as children use language to make sense of their world. According to Vygotsky (1978), much of what children learn occurs within the context of their social interactions with others, and it is through these interactions that they develop language facility. As children's language facility increases, they become more competent language users. Language in turn helps to organize and guide thinking and becomes a key factor in children's development of higher cognitive processes.

In what has become a cornerstone of his theory, Vygotsky (1978) makes a distinction between actual development and potential development. Actual development refers to the level at which children can complete a learning task independently, while potential development is the level at which they might be capable of completing a learning task with assistance. The distance between the two is known as the *zone of proximal development*. Vygotsky explains the zone of proximal development as:

> the distance between the actual developmental level as determined by independent problem solving and the level of potential development as determined through problem solving under adult guidance or in collaboration with more capable peers. (Vygotsky, 1978: 84)

According to Vygotsky, children become independent learners as they engage in challenging and meaningful tasks. Vygotsky further points out that it is through the support and scaffolding of parents and teachers that this cognitive growth is facilitated.

Given the social dimension of learning, teachers are encouraged to plan instructional experiences that foster social interaction. This is particularly effective when working with ELLs. Likewise, the facilitative role that the teacher has in scaffolding students' learning based on their zone of proximal development is emphasized in the sociocultural perspective.

Reading and writing are meaning-making processes that are influenced by the social contexts in which they occur. An example of literacy instruction in which we also see connections to constructivism is Reader Response Theory. Reader Response theorists explain that meaning is created during reading as the reader's background knowledge and experiences transact with the author's words. According to Rosenblatt (1991), readers read for two basic purposes or stances: *efferently* (for information) and *aesthetically* (for enjoyment or pleasure). Rosenblatt reminds us, though, that often readers use a combination of these two stances.

This overview of the dimensions of literacy and how they fit into the constructivist perspective of literacy is depicted in Figure 2.1. As the figure illustrates, the intertwining of features from the psycholinguistic, interactive, and sociocultural perspectives all contribute to form the constructionist view of literacy.

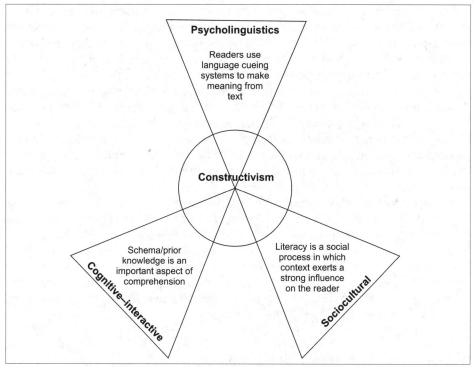

Figure 2.1 Literacy perspectives and constructivism

THE NATURE OF SECOND LANGUAGE ACQUISITION

The process of acquiring a second language is complex, and requires considerable time and multiple experiences. While there are certain parallels with first language (L1) acquisition, second language (L2) learning has unique characteristics. Among these differences are that L2 learners are more cognitively developed, have a store of linguistic knowledge in L1, and are able to use their experience of learning the first language to facilitate learning in the second language (Carrasquillo, 1994). In this section, we address two critical issues that impact second language learners: (1) comprehensible input and the affective filter and (2) interpersonal and academic language.

Comprehensible Input and the Affective Filter

In the works of Krashen (1982) and Terrell (1981), we see a conceptualization of second language acquisition that considers an innate creative construction process as universal to all languages. The acquisition of grammatical structures by the second language learner proceeds in a 'natural' predictable order. Acquisition occurs unconsciously without the learner's concern for rules and grammatical structures. Acquisition is dependent to a large degree on what is called 'comprehensible input'(Krashen, 1981; Long, 1981), this is linguistic input that is slightly beyond the learner's level of L2 mastery but is not too difficult for the learner to understand. It is through exposure to this 'comprehensible input' that the learner will acquire more complex and sophisticated language. Conscious learning, which differs from acquisition, occurs when the learner has sufficient mastery of the language structures and can apply them in a conscious manner. In the acquisition of a second language, individuals move through several stages, beginning with a preproduction stage in which they begin to understand but produce little spoken language. Learners advance in natural stages until they reach what is called the fluency/proficiency stage.

The affective filter plays an important role in second language acquisition (Dulay & Burt, 1977; Krashen, 1982). By definition, the affective filter is based on the idea that the learner's emotional state or attitude acts as an adjustable 'filter' that either promotes or impedes language acquisition. Learners with a 'low affective filter' seek and receive more input in the second language, show more confidence in interacting with their peers, and reach higher levels of proficiency. Learners who, because of fear or embarrassment, have high affective filters, are impeded in making progress in learning the new language.

Interpersonal and Academic Language

Cummins (1994, 2001) has offered a conceptualization of second language acquisition and proficiency that includes both social and academic language. The social language skills, which Cummins initially referred to as basic interpersonal communication skills or BICS, is the kind of language needed to carry on a conversation at a party or join in a game on the playground. This type of language occurs within a communicative event and is often supported by other cues such as facial expressions, intonation, gestures, and body language. Cummins describes this language as context-embedded and more recently (2001) has used the term 'contextualized language' when referring to BICS. Contextualized language or BICS, which includes the skills needed for oral fluency and sociolinguistic appropriateness, is usually quickly acquired.

The academic language, initially identified as Cognitive Academic Language Proficiency or CALP, is the language students most often meet in school. This language is generally considered context-reduced because the learner is not supported by interpersonal and contextual cues but must rather rely on linguistic cues to meaning. Included in CALP, which Cummins now refers to as decontextualized language, are literacy skills needed for academic work.

Cummins' framework of second language proficiency is represented in Figure 2.2 as the intersection of two continua. One continuum relates to the amount of contextual support available to language users as they engage in expressive and receptive meaning making. The intersecting continuum represents the level of

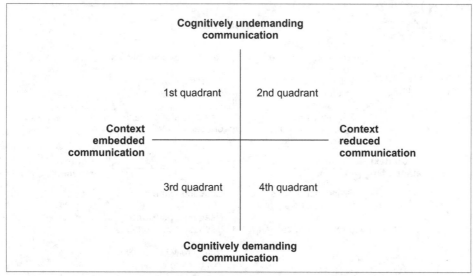

Figure 2.2 Cummins' framework of second language proficiency

Source: Baker (2001: 172)

cognitive demand that is placed on individuals as they process information and complete a communicative task. Each quadrant depicted in the figure represents the intersection of varying levels of linguistic support and cognitive demands. Examples of specific communicative activities that fall within each of these quadrants are provided in Figure 2.3.

To account for how second language learners can use knowledge gained in one language to support learning in another language, Cummins proposed the 'Interdependence Hypothesis'. According to Cummins (1984), because there is a Common Underlying Proficiency (CUP) that goes across languages – a reciprocal relationship exists between languages. This relationship enables learning in one language to 'transfer' to the other. However, transfer of knowledge from one language to the other can take place only if the learner has reached a specific 'linguistic threshold' of proficiency (Baker & Jones, 1998).

ISSUES INVOLVED IN PLANNING INSTRUCTION FOR ENGLISH LANGUAGE LEARNERS

As schools work to meet the challenge that comes with the increase in the number of ELLs in mainstream classrooms, it is essential to have an understanding of some of the issues that underlie current practices. How instruction is planned, organized, and provided for ELLs is strongly influenced by the individual teacher's perception of the relationship between L2 oral proficiency and L2 literacy functioning.

	Cognitively undemanding	
	Greeting someone	Reciting nursery rhymes
	Talking about the weather today	Listening to a story or poem on cassette
	Make their own books based on their own spoken or written stories	Describe stories heard or seen on TV
Context embedded		**Context reduced**
	Giving instructions about making a painting	Listening to the news
	Use simple measuring skills	Reading a book and discussing the contents
	Role play	Relate new information in a book to existing knowledge
	Dramatic stories	
	Solution seeking	Discuss ways that language is written; styles and conventions
	Explaining and justifying	Reflecting on feelings
	Cognitively demanding	

Figure 2.3 Examples of communicative activities
Source: Baker (2001: 176)

Although English verbal abilities are not necessarily an accurate indicator of an individual's actual level of knowledge, the perception often is that lack of L2 oral proficiency inhibits students' ability to participate in interactive learning tasks. This frequently leads teachers to engage in a passive instructional style that offers few opportunities for students to develop more sophisticated language and higher-level thinking skills. Such literacy instruction is teacher-directed, with ELLs spending a minimal amount of time reading and more time listening and watching the teacher (Neufeld & Fitzgerald, 2001; Padron, 1994; Ramirez *et al.*, 1991). This occurs because teachers view mastery of the surface features of the second language as a prerequisite to more complex linguistic and cognitive functioning. By surface features of language, we mean *phonology* (the sound system of the language), *morphology* (the system for building words), *syntax* (the word order or grammar of the language), and *lexical knowledge* (the collection of words and meanings that make up the language). As an example, children's correct pronunciation and grammar usage are seen as indicators of their ability to understand such subjects as science and social studies.

Instructional decisions are made on that presumption. The scenarios displayed below and on the following page illustrate how differing teacher perceptions influence instructional styles.

Scenario 1: Ms Allen's Literacy Class

Ms Allen's third-grade classroom is a busy room where the students are engaged in various literacy activities. Classroom library books and other materials are available for the children's use throughout the day. About half of the children are native speakers of English, and the others are bilingual speakers of Spanish and English. The children are grouped for literacy instruction according to their abilities. The groups are set at the beginning of the year, but there is flexibility and children may be moved 'up' or 'down' from one group to another. Juanita is a new student in Ms Allen's class. She recently arrived from Ecuador, and has limited knowledge of English. Juanita has been placed in the low reading group with four other students, all of whom are considered to be struggling readers. Two of these students are bilinguals who have been in the school from one to two years but are still identified as ELLs based on the criteria for determining English language proficiency as established by the school district. Everyone in the class is encouraged to use English all the time. Most of the literacy instructional time for Juanita's group is spent on decoding practice and reading from simplified materials in round-robin style and choral-reading fashion. This work is reinforced through the completion of accompanying worksheets. Correct pronunciation of reading vocabulary is a high priority and Ms Allen spends considerable time working on this. This group uses a template for journal writing that requires them to insert the appropriate missing words each day. Juanita and the other two bilingual students also receive instruction from the ESL teacher in a pull-out program of instruction.

In contrast to the 'low reading group' in Ms Allen's class, the other literacy instructional groups work with both literature-based basal materials and trade books. Ms Allen uses a variety of instructional modes with these students, including guided reading, buddy reading, and independent reading. Response to reading may be through discussion, journal writing, or extended projects. These students do not use the template in their journal writing, and generally write in response to a prompt.

Ms Allen is a caring teacher who is concerned about providing appropriate instruction for all the students in her class, but believes that the 'low' group would not be capable of engaging in the same types of instructional activities as the other students. She also believes that the students in the 'low' group will derive the most benefit from the repetitive type of instructional format.

Scenario 2: Ms Jackson's Literacy Class

Ms Jackson's fourth-grade classroom is a bustling place where students can be observed working in various configurations during the literacy instructional block. The class is presently working on a thematic unit on rainforests, and related materials have been strategically placed in centers around the room. As in Ms Allen's class, about half of the children are native speakers of English and the others are either Spanish/English or Vietnamese/English bilingual speakers. The children are working in groups that are based on their literacy projects for the theme unit. Throughout the year, the groupings change and Ms Jackson often forms small groups for mini-lessons based on her assessment of the students' needs. Posters hanging around the room detail classroom procedures as well as literacy strategies. Whenever possible, Ms Jackson tries to provide visuals to accompany the print on the posters, and this enables the ELLs with limited English literacy proficiency to participate in activities. Ms Jackson believes that her role is to scaffold learning situations for her students, but she also encourages them to develop a sense of their own independent abilities. Two of the ELLs, Carlos and Lily, have limited English knowledge. The other bilingual students have been in the school longer and have acquired more English, but they are still identified as ELLs according to the district testing data. Like the other students in the class, Carlos and Lily participate in the various group activities. At times, they work as a duo with Ms Jackson, while at other times Ms Jackson meets with them individually to provide them with additional support. Other students from their respective language groups also help Carlos and Lily, sometimes translating Ms Jackson's instructions for them. Ms Jackson has signs posted in the classroom that are written in English, Spanish, and Vietnamese. The English speakers enjoy trying to learn the words in the other languages and, when they see the posted signs, the bilingual children feel that their native languages are valued by the teacher.

Carlos and Lily receive ESL instruction in a pull-out program and Ms Jackson tries to make accommodations so that they will not feel left out of the activities that the class is engaged in while they are out of the room. Sometimes this means that Ms Jackson will make an audiotape of a book that the class has read so that Carlos and Lily can follow along as a read aloud; at other times, English-proficient students may work with them.

Overall, Carlos and Lily have the opportunity to be exposed to the same high-level content as the rest of the class. The difference is that they need more support, which Ms Jackson arranges for them to have. They also have the opportunity for peer interaction throughout the day. Ms Jackson believes that lack of English oral proficiency should not mean that a student is deprived of grade level content material. She also thinks that the best way for her students to gain proficiency in English is to be exposed to language use in meaningful situations.

The two scenarios presented here illustrate the debate among those who are responsible for providing instruction for ELLs in the mainstream classroom. As we saw in the first scenario, Ms Allen viewed the ELL students as needing to increase their English oral proficiency before engaging in English literacy learning tasks that would foster making meaning from text. The converse was the case in the second scenario, where Ms Jackson understood English oral proficiency and literacy to be interrelated and interdependent. For this reason, she believed that exposing her ELLs to English reading and writing would support both their oral and their written English development. As was also shown in Scenario 1, Ms Allen's method of instruction relied strongly on teacher-directed activities and repetition of oral language forms when working with the ELL students. This supported Ms Allen's perception that the components of a second language are learned in a hierarchical fashion, that is, proficiency in oral language (speaking and listening) must occur before written language can be dealt with. In contrast, Ms Jackson's use of partner grouping in which English-proficient students were paired with ELL students enabled the ELL students to participate in class activities that would provide a context for increasing their oral skills while at the same time affording them the opportunity to engage in more meaningful literacy tasks.

The two scenarios reflect what actually occurs in many classrooms where mainstream teachers are faced with the challenge of providing effective instruction for ELLs. Although researchers have examined the question of how influential oral language proficiency is to literacy development, there is no consensus on the level of L2 oral proficiency that ELLs need to have before they can engage in reading and writing in the second language (see Garcia, 2000 for a review). While some studies (e.g. Verhoeven, 1994) have shown that students are able to learn second language reading and writing and develop their oral proficiency at the same time, others, such as Schmidt (1993), found that lack of L2 oral proficiency impeded progress in literacy development. In addition, after conducting research, Bernhardt and Kamil (1995) 'concluded that second-language reading is a function of L1 reading ability and second-language grammatical ability' (Bernhardt, 2000: 803). Another question is the role that the first/native language plays in L2 literacy development. Initially, L1 influence on second language ability was often regarded negatively as interfering with second language learning. Although it has been shown that using both languages can have a facilitating effect on comprehension (Jimenez, 1992; Jimenez et al., 1995, 1996), use of the first language is still looked on as an impediment in many classrooms.

CONCLUSION

In this chapter, we have examined the various dimensions that have contributed to the constructivist perspective of literacy, in which readers and writers are seen as making meaning through written language. The constructivist perspective forms the basis for the instructional strategies presented throughout this book. As meaning-makers, students in constructivist classrooms take an active role in their own learning.

As we have sought to describe the characteristics of constructivism, we have focused on three dimensions: the psycholinguistic dimension, the cognitive-interactive dimension, and the sociocultural dimension. The psycholinguists have helped us to see readers and writers as language users, who tap into their linguistic abilities to use the syntactic, semantic, and graphophonemic cueing systems to generate meaning. The cognitive dimension has given us a 'window' into how readers and writers process written language. From cognitive psychology, we have gained an understanding of the important role that background knowledge or schema plays as individuals interact with text-based information to construct meaning. The sociocultural dimension of literacy accounts for our understanding that literacy events are influenced by the social and cultural contexts in which they occur. This dimension supports our belief that students' literacy learning can be facilitated by providing literacy experiences that foster social interaction.

In our discussion of L2 acquisition, we noted that this process is complex and requires considerable time to occur. Increasingly complex and sophisticated language is acquired through the 'comprehensible input' that a learner is exposed to. Also influencing L2 acquisition is the learner's emotional state and attitude or 'affective filter'. This affective filter can either promote or impede language acquisition.

We have also described L2 acquisition and proficiency in terms of the demands of social language and academic language. Social language develops within a relatively short time and is supported by context and non-linguistic cues. Academic language, which is what students meet most often in school, is more abstract and is not supported by interpersonal and contextual cues. Becoming proficient in academic language requires a much longer period of time.

ELLs' lack of oral language proficiency has often hindered their opportunity to receive cognitively-stimulating and content-level appropriate instruction in school. We again want to stress the positive relationship that exists between providing meaningful literacy and content area tasks for ELLs and their academic and cognitive growth.

Moving Beyond the Transition: Struggling English Literacy Learners in the Regular/Mainstream Classroom

Introduction

Varied Backgrounds, Varied Abilities,
and Varied Needs

Monolingual and Bilingual Literacy
Learners

Emergent, Transitional and
Developmental Issues

Literacy Demands in the Upper
Elementary Grades

Conclusion

CHAPTER 3

Moving Beyond the Transition: Struggling English Literacy Learners in the Regular/ Mainstream Classroom

INTRODUCTION

As we mentioned in Chapter 1, if any doubts existed, the 2000 US census confirmed for demographers what many teachers already knew: multilingual students are found in schools throughout the entire United States. Regardless of geographical region (southwest, midwest, urban, suburban, rural), or socioeconomic status (poor, middle class, wealthy) teachers are encountering significant numbers of English language learners (ELLs) in their classrooms. This increase in linguistic diversity comes at a time when many states and school districts are drastically limiting the kinds of instructional support provided to multilingual learners. Many students with limited English oral and written language abilities are being swiftly transferred into regular or mainstream classrooms. In fact, according to Neufeld and Fitzgerald (2001), the vast majority of English language learners are in English-only classrooms.

There is a substantial body of literature on teaching both oral and written English to children whose home language is other than English (e.g. Freeman & Freeman, 1994; Peregoy & Boyle, 1997; Rigg & Allen, 1989). Historically, these children have been the focus of both the educational and the academic community. Teachers and researchers, however, have a far more limited understanding of students who are 'beyond the transition' (Goldenberg, 1996) – students who have moved from bilingual or English as a second language (ESL) instructional contexts to monolingual English instructional settings. Although 'transitioned,' a substantial number of these students continue to experience difficulty with academic English literacy throughout their school careers (Gersten, 1996). And it has been well documented that literacy abilities are highly correlated with academic success and school retention rates (Garcia, 1992).

These difficulties are compounded by the fact that in upper elementary grades – where many of these students are found – literacy becomes the primary mode of transmitting information. In such fields as science and the social sciences, students encounter academic discourses and disciplinary concepts that go beyond the more familiar literary and personal narrative. The demands of cognitive academic language (Cummins, 1980, 2001) significantly increase. Even in literature, picture books, short stories, and 'one sitting' readings are replaced by extended 'chapter books' that are independently read across space and time. Finally, teacher talk, which during the early grades was conversational and informal in nature, becomes more presentational and formal, often taking on the characteristics of a lecture.

Accompanying this increased emphasis on learning through literacy is a decreased emphasis on literacy instruction. Many teachers in the upper elementary grades assume – or hope – that the literacy 'basics' have already been taught and mastered. Little instructional support is provided to students, regardless of their language status, as they make their way through various academic discourses. ELLs, therefore, are frequently in monolingual English school settings with teachers who do not know how to promote their literacy development. When literacy needs are addressed, a remedial model is often used. The focus is on teaching letter and sound correspondences or vocabulary, a replication of what the students may have already experienced in previous grades. Unfortunately, such models are typically ineffective with 'transitioned' students (Gersten, 1996) because they fail to address their instructional needs.

We begin this chapter with a look at the varied linguistic, cognitive, sociocultural, and academic characteristics of students who have 'moved beyond the transition.' Beyond the transition, as we use the phrase, refers to students who have previously received both oral and written ESL (English as a second language) instruction in language assistance programs. The linguistic and cognitive abilities of transitioned students may have been developed within bilingual or ESL classrooms or through pull-out programs. Such students bring to the classroom a developing understanding of spoken and written English. As part of our discussion of ELLs, we investigate the similarities and differences between transitioned students and monolingual English learners. Although transitioned students have unique needs, they also have much in common with their fellow monolingual classmates. The chapter concludes with an examination of the emergent, transitional, and developmental issues that impact English language learners and the unique literacy demands they encounter in intermediate grades (grades 4 to 6).

VARIED BACKGROUNDS, VARIED ABILITIES, AND VARIED NEEDS

Attempting to characterize the background of the English language learners is a difficult task at best. Diversity within the ELL community is the norm. Even within a classroom where students all speak the same home language, linguistic and educational variation among the students is often prevalent. Our purpose, therefore, is to provide teachers with a general understanding of the linguistic and cognitive abilities of the English language learners sitting in their classrooms. At the same time, however, we must also acknowledge that some students may not fit the 'norm' being described. There will always be students who are the exception to the rule. Additionally, our emphasis here is on abilities, not deficits. Too often the capabilities and experiences that English language learners bring to the classroom are unnoticed because the focus is on what they lack or what they need to learn.

Many English language learners in the intermediate grades are in the process of developing two languages, the language of the home and that of the school. As we explained in Chapter 1, it may be that a non-English language is used exclusively in the child's home, just as English may be used exclusively in the classroom. Such students may be recent immigrants to the United States and/or come from families where the parents have not yet developed English. This does not mean, however, that students from monolingual non-English homes are unaware of English before they attend school. Except in the most isolated of situations, many children informally encounter spoken English through such media as television and radio.

It is often the case that two languages are spoken in the home, although not necessarily by all family members. Parents, for example, may be monolingual in a non-English language but older siblings bring English into the home as a result of their school experiences. The younger children are therefore introduced to English by their siblings before reaching school age, and may come to interact with their parents in the home language and with their older, schooled siblings in English.

It is important to acknowledge as well as to stress that all children, regardless of linguistic background, bring into the school a developing control over at least one spoken language. Children do not enter the instructional context without knowing how to talk. Those fortunate children who have encountered two languages in the home bring developing knowledge of two languages to the classroom. Despite what is popularly believed, these children do not confuse the two languages. Rather, from the very beginning, they develop two separate linguistic systems and know when to appropriately use each language within various communicative contexts (Edelsky, 1986; Genesse, 1989; Hornberger, 1989). When code switching (using two languages in a communicative setting) does occur, it is frequently because students lack the vocabulary in the second language or because the person being talked to knows both languages.

The introduction of literacy (reading and writing) complicates and enriches the relationship between the home and the school language. There may be children in the classroom who have developed some facility with both the written and the oral form of the home language. In most cases, these biliterate abilities have been developed within school contexts. Biliteracy may have been learned formally in a school setting in another country, or through bilingual programs in the United States. Of course, students may not be equally proficient in the two languages. It is most likely that the biliterate students will be better able to use the home written language in some contexts and the English written language in others.

In some circumstances, students may not know the written form of their home language. They may have been in ESL programs in the school that did not teach literacy in the home language, or else come from countries in which schooling was not available. Even here, however, the children may have informally developed some knowledge of the written form of their home language. Books, magazines, and letters written in the home language may have been encountered in the home. Environmental print found on food products, on advertisements, or in stores within the community can also contribute to an understanding of literacy in the home language. There will also be some students who come to the classroom having little knowledge of literacy in either language. This does not mean that they are unaware of the written language system, just that they have not yet had the opportunity to develop control over the system.

Regardless of which background the child brings to the classroom, it is important to acknowledge that no child enters the classroom without having been part of a linguistic community. In fact, it is as a member of such a community that the child has developed spoken language. Linguistically, these children are not 'blank slates' waiting to be taught language. Rather, transitioned ELLs bring to the classroom a well-developed understanding of the home language and a developing under-standing of oral and written English. This does not mean that the students' spoken and written English will not continue to grow and develop, but this is true for monolingual English students as well. The speech of a first grader is very different from that of a sixth grader. Oral language development continues regardless of the language background. It is important to keep these linguistic abilities in mind when instructing English language learners. Teachers will be better able to build upon the linguistic facility of these students, even if there has been little English develop-ment, if they look for, acknowledge, and affirm what the student is able to do linguistically rather than look only for what is missing.

MONOLINGUAL AND BILINGUAL LITERACY LEARNERS: SOMETHING OLD, SOMETHING NEW, SOMETHING BORROWED ...

Traditionally, most attention for promoting literacy development, regardless of language, has focused on younger children. The adage, 'children learn to read and write in their first years of school and then use reading and writing for learning in the later years' has encouraged this focus. Teachers of intermediate-grade students, therefore, concentrate their instructional attention on the content found in the various disciplines, such as social studies, science, and mathematics. Suggestions that they are also teachers of literacy are frequently met with resistance. When ELLs are added to the intermediate classroom mix, teachers may feel overwhelmed.

English language learners certainly do add to the instructional demands of teachers. These demands, however, become more manageable when we under-

Table 3.1 Similarities and differences between monolingual and transitioned English literacy learners.

Monolingual English literacy learners	Transitioned English literacy learners
Knowledge of and experiences with the world.	Knowledge of and experiences with the world.
Conceptual knowledge is strongly linked to the English language.	Conceptual knowledge may be strongly linked to the home language and to a much lesser degree to English.
Multiple experiences using spoken and written English in school contexts.	Fewer experiences using spoken and written English in school contexts.
Well-established, yet still developing, knowledge of spoken and written English.	Developing knowledge of spoken and written English.
Fewer experiences using spoken and written English in such disciplines as the sciences and social sciences.	Fewer experiences using spoken and written English in such disciplines as the sciences and social sciences.
Make use of various strategies for generating meaning.	Make use of various strategies for generating meaning, but more slowly.
Make use of metacognitive strategies to monitor their reading and writing.	Make use of metacognitive strategies to monitor their reading and writing, but more slowly.
Make use of context when reading.	Less use of context when reading.
Can only rely on knowledge of English to facilitate an understanding of English.	May rely on the home language to facilitate an understanding of English.

stand how ELLs are similar – something old – as well as different – something new – from their monolingual English-speaking peers. Additionally, ELLs are often able to 'borrow' what they have learned in their home language and use it when interacting with English. Once these similarities, differences, and borrowings are identified, teachers can build on and extend these commonalities among students and at the same time find ways to address the differences. Table 3.1 sets forth some of the critical similarities and differences between monolingual and transitioned English literacy learners.

It is well established that all readers and writers, regardless of language abilities, use their background knowledge when interacting with written language. In fact, knowledge of the content being read or written about is one of the most powerful factors in determining how well a text will be read or written (Fitzgerald, 1995; Kucer, 2001; Tierney & Pearson, 1994). Just as all students bring some language facility with them to the classroom, so too do they bring background knowledge. It may be the case that the students' prior experiences are not culturally congruent with those of the school, or that they lack well-developed knowledge of particular school subjects. However, no child is an empty vessel waiting to filled by the classroom teacher.

Not only must teachers acknowledge the experience these students bring to the classroom, but they must encourage students to use it (Garcia, 2000). Frequently, because the language and the culture of the school may conflict with the language and culture of their homes, ELLs are hesitant to draw upon their experiences. They simply assume that their knowledge is of no relevance in the school setting. Unconditional acceptance of the relevance of the students' histories will help students to apply what they know about the world to their reading and writing. The sharing of these histories will also enrich the life of the classroom.

There will be instances in which ELLs may lack knowledge of the content under study. Of course, this is also true for monolingual English-speaking students. In these cases, the curriculum must help students build an understanding of the content through multiple and varied experiences with it. A single exposure to the content simply will not be adequate. The impact of background knowledge on the reading and writing processes is one reason why the use of thematic units or an integrated curricula have been promoted for both bilingual and monolingual students (e.g. Silva & Delgado-Larocco, 1993; Kucer, et al., 1995). In thematic units, there is a continual building up of interrelated linguistic and concept knowledge from which students can draw when reading and writing. This development of knowledge occurs not only over space and time, but also through varied experiences that include oral and written language and such communication systems as art, music, and movement.

Frequently, the conceptual knowledge – what Moll and Greenberg (1990) have referred to as 'funds of knowledge' – of bilingual students goes unnoticed. As previously noted, one reason for this is the discontinuity between school and home knowledge, values, and culture. A second reason is related to the strong link between conceptual knowledge and language. Much of what we have learned about the world has been developed through the use of language. When sharing with others what we know, the language through which that knowledge was generated is used as a base for communication. When there is a match between the language used for knowledge development and the language used for communication (e.g. I communicate knowledge initially generated through the use of English in English) my entrée to the knowledge is relatively easy. However, if I share the same knowledge through the use of another language (e.g. Spanish) my accessing and processing of the knowledge may take longer and may be more demanding.

Because of these additional processing demands, many bilingual students may appear to be less knowledgeable simply because they need extra time to formulate in English the ideas that they initially encountered in another language. Added to this challenge is the fact that bilingual students may have a firm grasp of the concept under study, but lack the English vocabulary for talking about it. This lack of vocabulary often forces bilingual students to 'talk around the idea' because they lack the language to directly address the issue. More so than with monolingual students, it therefore becomes imperative that teachers extend their wait time when interacting with ELLs.

This need for additional processing time is directly linked to the fact that transitioned ELLs have usually had far fewer experiences of using spoken and written English within school contexts than have their monolingual counterparts. For monolingual students, English is a well-established and developed communication system. They have had numerous opportunities to employ the language – especially narrative – in a variety of settings within the classroom. Although their oral and written language continues to develop, they typically control basic semantic, syntactic, and graphophonemic patterns. The bilingual students, on the other hand, are still developing such control. They will need additional rich and meaningful linguistic experiences that allow for talking and listening in English. The continued promotion of spoken language abilities will ultimately promote written language abilities. We know that oral English abilities have a pervasive and lasting effect on literacy achievement (Mace-Matluck *et al.*, 1989). Fortunately, because advances in written language promote spoken language development, and progress in spoken language supports written language development (Hudelson, 1994), there is no need to sequence the use of the two language modes within the classroom.

For both monolingual and transitioned students, much of the language as well as the content encountered in the intermediate grades may be relatively new to them. As students reach the upper grades, social studies and the sciences begin to play a more prominent role in the curriculum. The specialized ways with words (Schoenbach, *et al.*, 1999; Greenleaf *et al.*, 2001) and the specialized ways of thinking within these disciplines may cause problems for both groups of students. Therefore, what students have learned about literacy in the early grades will not automatically transfer to these content areas. Additionally, because even the literary texts encountered through reading and writing increase significantly in length, students may lack adequate 'repair strategies' to help them work their way through processing difficulties. Dilemmas that students were able to ignore in shorter texts become increasingly problematic with longer texts. These new processing demands require that teachers show, demonstrate, and make visible to students how literacy operates within the academic disciplines. Simply telling them will not suffice (Jimenez & Gersten, 1999).

Most transitioned students in the mainstream classroom will also have, as well their monolingual classmates, a basic understanding of many of the processes involved in spoken and written English. They have learned or are learning various strategies for generating meaning through and from print (Fitzgerald, 1995; Mace-Matluck *et al.*, 1989). However, the transitioned students will typically access and use these strategies more slowly than monolingual English students. It will take them longer to read and write, not necessarily because the strategies are unavailable to them, but because they have less control over them. Both groups of students will also have the ability to use context when reading, although the bilingual students may tend to make use of context less frequently or less effectively. This may be partially due to the fact that transitioned students more frequently encounter words that they do not know or do not recognize. The use of context for word identification is most effective when all the words surrounding the word are known. For bilingual students this may not be the case, and there may be several words within a single sentence that are new to them.

It may also be the case that some bilingual students will have limited processing strategies available to them. This limitation may be displayed in the more frequent meaning-disrupting miscues often found in ELLs' reading (Fitzgerald, 1995). Often, initial English literacy instruction for bilingual students emphasizes decoding skills as the basis for reading and writing. In such instructional contexts, the ability to 'sound out' as the basis for word identification and spelling overrides the teaching and learning of other strategies such as the use of context, read on and return, monitoring for meaning and brainstorming techniques for accessing ideas. These students will need continued support in developing additional strategies to help them to move effectively through written language (Kucer, 1995). However, it is still possible to comprehend the 'big ideas' in a text, even if some words are unrecognized. Bilingual students frequently a great facility for piecing together a general understanding despite the gaps in their processing abilities.

Although ELLs have had fewer experiences with English than their monolingual counterparts, they do have myriad experiences with the language of the home. First-language knowledge, rather than simply interfering with the second language, can also be used as a support. That is, first language can be applied to the second (Edelsky, 1986). Cognates (words that are comparable in both languages, such as the Spanish words 'producto', 'record' for the English words 'product', 'record'), similar syntactic and semantic sentence structures, and shared discourse organizational patterns can all be employed by the bilingual student in the use of English. In such instances, aspects of the first language transfer onto the second.

EMERGENT, TRANSITIONAL, AND DEVELOPMENTAL ISSUES FOR ENGLISH LITERACY LEARNERS

In general, ELLs develop literacy in ways that are highly similar to those of monolingual learners (Bernhardt, 2000; Neufeld & Fitzgerald, 2001; Peregoy & Boyle, 1997). As observed by Hudelson (1994), ELLs are actively engaged in constructing hypotheses for how the language operates. Students who have been transitioned have formed hypotheses and understandings about the relationship between print, sound, and meaning. In general, during the emergence of literacy, they have developed knowledge about various purposes and functions of literacy and such conventions as punctuation and capitalization. They also understand how speech can be segmented into phonemes, and how these individual sounds are linked to the letters of the alphabet.

Building on their evolving understanding of surface-level conventions of written language, English language learners are also acquiring self-monitoring strategies for generating meaning. They ask themselves if what they have read or written makes sense, and continue to develop a knowledge of letters, sounds, spelling patterns, and words that supports them in this sense-making process. They also are increasingly able to apply what they know about their spoken language (such as syntax) to written discourse (Neufeld & Fitzgerald, 2001).

What is somewhat unique about transitioned students is the degree of anxiety that they may experience when they enter mainstream classrooms (Pappamihiel, 2002). They may avoid monolingual English-speaking students and be reluctant to enter into classroom discussions. Interestingly, this anxiety is not necessarily linked to the students' actual proficiency in English, but rather to perceived proficiency. Students believing they lack the cognitive and linguistic knowledge necessary for proficient English use tend to experience high levels of anxiety. Girls are frequently more anxious than boys.

High levels of anxiety can thwart continued English-literacy learning because it inhibits risk-taking and hypothesis formation. Literacy learning and development involves the active engagement of the learner who is attempting to form an understanding of how the language operates. When students feel threatened by the instructional context, this active engagement lessens significantly. Students become more concerned with simply 'getting through' the activity with as little embarrassment as possible, regardless of the success they may or may not experience.

Teachers can reduce anxiety in English language students by allowing them more time to answer questions. This will allow students the necessary time to formulate their answers in a language with which they are still struggling. Allowing students to use their home language with their classmates and reducing the number of times they are required to respond in front of the entire class can also lessen anxiety.

LITERACY DEMANDS IN THE UPPER ELEMENTARY GRADES

As students move into the upper elementary grades, the nature of classroom instruction and texts begins to change. Texts and literacy practices become increasingly specialized within the disciplines. Consequently, literacy abilities that were functional in the primary grades may suddenly become inadequate. As reflected in Table 3.2, all intermediate children, regardless of linguistic background or schooling experiences, confront very different kinds of reading and writing.

Perhaps one of the biggest differences between literacy use in the primary and upper elementary grades, as well as one of the most significant challenges for both students and teachers, is the increase the length of texts and the time spent reading and writing them. Whereas in the early grades students tend to read or write a text in one sitting, in the upper grades, owing to their increased length, texts may be read and written over space and time. No longer can a student who is struggling with reading or writing a text simply discard it, knowing that tomorrow a new text will appear. Rather, problems with a particular text one day will often be problems the following day. This challenge is compounded by the fact that textbooks in the content areas become a primary vehicle through which teaching and learning take place (Alvermann & Phelps, 1998).

In addition to the challenge of text length is the fact that many teachers in the upper elementary grades view reading and writing as processes through which

Table 3.2 Primary and intermediate literacy demands

Primary (kindergarten – third grade)	Intermediate (fourth – eighth grade)
A focus on learning to read and write.	A focus on reading and writing to learn.
Reading and writing short texts in one sitting: single-episode short stories, folk/fairy tales, limericks, tongue twisters, etc.	Reading and writing of longer texts and chapter books, which occurs across space and time; multiple-episode short stories, novels, chapter text books; etc.
The range of texts read and written is narrow and texts tend to be personal narratives or imaginative in nature.	The range of texts read and written widens and texts are increasingly informative in nature.
Reading and writing from a single source.	Reading and writing from multiple sources; new literacy demands such as note-taking and research report.
The text structures read and written are in a time-order sequence.	The read and written text structures widen to include not only time order, but also compare and contrast, problem and solution, cause and effect, and idea development.
Sentences read and written tend to be simple semantic and syntactic structures.	Sentences read and written become more varied, reflecting complex semantic and syntactic structures.
A limited range of vocabulary is encountered, based largely on the child's spoken language.	A wider range of vocabulary is encountered; more use of technical and disciplinary terms and concepts not found in child's spoken language.
Reading and writing about known concepts and ideas.	Reading and writing about new concepts and ideas.
A focus on literature.	A focus on additional disciplines such as science, social science, and the use of mathematical story problems.
More teacher responsibility for student–text transaction.	More student responsibility for student–text transaction.

learning occurs. The focus shifts from learning to read and write to reading and writing to learn. This does not mean that all reading and writing instruction ceases, but that such instruction is not typically extended into the content areas of the social sciences and sciences. Interestingly, this shift in instructional focus occurs just at the time when reading and writing in the content areas takes on increased importance in the school curriculum. In the earlier grades, students tend to read and write imaginative or personal narrative texts that are arranged in a time order sequence. Short stories, folktales, and language play through poems, limericks and the like are frequently encountered. In the upper elementary grades, the use of expository discourse becomes common place. Although some discourse forms (such as narratives and poetry) continue in the curriculum, their length increases significantly. Also, with the use of information texts, the type of text structures being read and written moves from a focus on time order to one of compare and contrast, problem and solution, cause and effect, and idea development. These structures are a challenge to all students, not only those who have been transitioned.

Not only does the content and structure of the texts read and written change in the intermediate grades, but so too does the nature of the sentences and the vocabulary. In the literature the student must read but especially in the sciences and social sciences, sentences become much more complex syntactically and contain a much wider range of vocabulary. As previously noted, much of this new language reflects concepts and ideas with which the students may not be familiar. This intertwining of new language structures and new concepts places new linguistic and cognitive demands on the students. For those students still unsteady with the English language, these demands can be overwhelming.

CONCLUSION

This chapter has addressed both the similarities between monolingual and bilingual students and the unique instructional needs of the transitioned English literacy learners. Although ELLs may have developed the so-called 'basics' by the time they reach the intermediate grades, they are still in the process of fine-tuning this knowledge. However, the linguistic and cognitive demands markedly increase for all students in the upper grades. These increased demands particularly impact on the transitioned English literacy learner and require additional mediational or supportive instructional structures on the part of the teacher. The nature of these supportive instructional experiences is addressed in the remaining chapters of this book.

CHAPTER 4

Instructional Writing Strategies for Struggling English Language Learners

Introduction

Mediating and Scaffolding
Writing Development

Writing in the Disciplines:
Moving Beyond Personal
Experiences and Narratives

Helping Students Organize
Text Structures

Helping Students Organize
Text Meanings

Conclusion

CHAPTER 4

Instructional Writing Strategies for Struggling English Language Learners

INTRODUCTION

Many transitioned upper elementary ELL students continue to experience difficulty with writing as they progress through school. As we discussed in Chapters 1 and 3, some of these challenges are unique to them as learners and some are related to the increased conceptual and linguistic demands of the upper elementary grades. In either case, these students are not beginning writers. At this point in their instructional histories, ELLs have had numerous encounters with written language and have developed some control over the so-called 'basics' of the writing process. They can appropriately use many of the conventions of written language, such as spelling, punctuation, and capitalization, and demonstrate increased control over sentence structure. Additionally, in the upper elementary grades, ELLs are fairly comfortable writing short narratives or stories and writing about their personal experiences. These abilities of the ELLs, however, are still in the process of being fine-tuned and may not yet be as well developed as those of their monolingual peers.

As discussed in Chapter 3, during the upper elementary grades there is an increasing focus on such critical and disciplinary-based written text structures as cause and effect, compare and contrast, and problem-solution. Writing activities that require the use and integration of multiple sources of information (texts) become commonplace and the length of writing assignments increases substantially. These unfamiliar writing activities place new linguistic and cognitive demands and stresses on English language learners who may still be a bit wobbly with the writing process. It also places new demands on the teacher who is called to provide the mediational support necessary for these learners. A return to the basics, an all-too-frequent response, will not adequately address the needs of these learners.

This chapter describes various mediational structures that support the writing development of English language learners. These mediational frameworks address the increased writing demands found in most upper elementary classrooms and also address the link between writing and the reading of content discourse and chapter books. Although a number of specific instructional writing activities are addressed, the primary focus is on how current or typical writing activities might be modified so as to meet the needs of the ELL student. Most teachers will find it difficult to construct separate and unique writing assignments for the English language student. However, the modification of existing activities is within their means, and such modifications will often be appropriate for the struggling monolingual students as well.

MEDIATING AND SCAFFOLDING WRITING DEVELOPMENT

Simply stated, instructional mediation is everything that teachers do to bring students to independence. In the case of writing and the English language learner, mediation is reflected in the instructional strategies that teachers implement to promote writing development in their bilingual learners. Vygotsky (1962, 1978) and others (e.g. Bruner, 1974; Wells, 1986; Wertsch, 1985) have proposed that the learning of complex cognitive activities, in this case writing, is first developed in social, collaborative contexts. More capable others, such as teachers, provide the support necessary for students to engage in activities that they would be unable to accomplish on their own. This social support activates the potential abilities of students, and allows them to begin the development of new forms of knowledge.

As illustrated in Figure 4.1, writing development is a process by which students move from potential to independent abilities. This developmental path of learning is traversed through varying degrees of scaffolding or support offered to the students by the teacher. Initially, when students are least capable, the teacher takes upon him or herself most dimensions of the writing process. Although the students may actually do very little of the writing, they observe the process made visible by the actions and talk of the teacher. As students come to understand the overall process through these teacher demonstrations, a part of the scaffold is deconstructed. The teacher no longer assumes responsibility for a particular aspect of writing, and the students are then expected to take up this feature. At this initial point, although the teacher may still be the primary writer, students have begun to engage in the process of writing as well.

This process of scaffold deconstruction and student assumption of increased responsibility continues until students are able to independently engage in the entire writing process without teacher support. That is, students are able to self-regulate their own writing. Abilities that were once social and collaborative in nature have become internalized and independent. Processes that were once visible are now largely hidden from sight.

For ELLs, the degree to which, and the length of time that, writing activities must

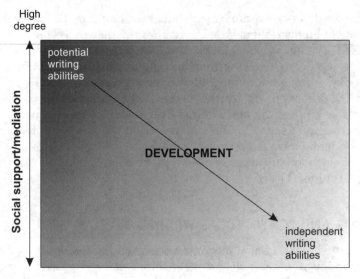

Figure 4.1 From collaborative to independent writing abilities

Adapted from Kucer (2001: 234)

be scaffolded will frequently be greater than for monolingual students. Scaffolds may initially need to be more extensive and last longer. A single presentation of how a writing activity is to be accomplished will usually not be effective. In Table 4.1 (Kucer & Silva, in progress), six general writing strategy lessons are presented. Each reflects a differing degree of support by the teacher, with the top strategy requiring the most support, and the bottom strategy requiring the least. Moving from to top strategy to the one, the teacher relinquishes more responsibility and the students assume greater control. These generic activities are presented because they are 'content free.' They can be used to teach a variety of kinds and forms of writing, and therefore can be easily adapted to a range of instructional contexts and a variety of students. A similar scaffolding framework for promoting reading development will be discussed in Chapter 5.

Teacher Writing

During teacher writing, the teacher demonstrates, both visually and verbally, the process of writing. On the chalkboard, overhead projector, or chart paper, the teacher writes a text that the students see evolve over space and time. As the writing unfolds, the teacher discusses his or her thinking processes that 'hide' behind the evolving text. In general, what the teacher chooses to discuss is determined by the activity itself, as well as by the ability of the students. The teacher, for example, may comment on idea selection and development, the choice and spelling of words, the structuring of sentences, or the use of punctuation and capitalization. The teacher

Table 4.1 Writing strategy lessons and mediation

MOST SUPPORT

Teacher writing

the teacher demonstrates the writing of a text,
discussing his/her thinking as s/he writes

Shared writing

the teacher records a text that the children dictate;
the teacher supports student generation of ideas by asking
questions and reflecting on text content,
development, organization, conventions, etc.

Choral writing

the teacher and the children write a text together;
the teacher and individual students take turns
generating and recording new ideas

Guided writing

individual children write a text, with the teacher
providing support by as necessary

Paired writing

two children write a text together

Independent writing
each child writes a text independently

LEAST SUPPORT

will possibly discuss self-monitoring behaviors, asking such questions as 'Does this make sense?' 'Does what I have written reflect my intentions as a writer?' 'Do I need to say more about this particular idea?' When revision occurs, the teacher makes visible for students both why the change is necessary, and how it is to be accomplished.

For ELLs being introduced to a new writing genre (such as comparing and contrasting two points of view, for example), teacher writing might involve the following:

(1) The two points of view are briefly shared with the students. This can be communicated on a three column T-chart in which the similarities between the two points of view are listed in the middle column. The right and left columns contain information that is unique to each perspective. As part of the sharing, the teacher might also note the various textual sources from which the information on the T-chart was taken.

(2)   The teacher selects those similarities and differences to be addressed in the writing, and discusses why they were chosen.
(3)   The teacher begins drafting the introduction, reflecting on the purpose of introductions in such types of writing (i.e. introductions frequently provide an overview of the information to be presented). The teacher also decides on the order of the information to be presented (will similarities or differences be presented first; in what order will similarities and differences be presented, etc.) and discusses his or her thinking with the students.
(4)   Writing about the first similarity or difference, the teacher cognitively shares the thinking processes and decisions that are driving the writing process. As in all of these steps, revisions are highlighted and shared with the students.
(5)   The teacher proceeds in this fashion, addressing all similarities or differences identified. Or, if the teacher believes that this will be sufficient for student understanding of this type of writing, he/she may decide to draft only one similarity and one difference.
(6)   As with the introduction, the teacher addresses the purpose of a conclusion and drafts one for the compare-and-contrast text that has been written.

Shared Writing

In shared writing, students generally take on the role of participant observers. The students dictate the ideas and language for the text and the teacher, acting as a scribe, records the text on the chalkboard, overhead projector, or chart paper. During this process, the teacher interacts with the students, asking questions about the content, development, and organization of ideas. As was the case during teacher writing, comments may also address written language conventions and students are prompted to self-monitor what is being written.

Continuing with our example of writing a compare-and-contrast text, shared writing might take on the following characteristics:

(1)   Before engaging in shared writing, the students have had some prior experience with compare-and-contrast texts., perhaps through teacher writing demonstrations and/or through reading and discussing published texts of this nature.
(2)   The students identify similarities and differences, and the teacher records these on a T-chart.
(3)   The teacher asks the students to select the points to be compared and contrasted. Why these points are selected and the order in which they are to be addressed are discussed.
(4)   The teacher engages the students in a discussion of the introduction and asks various students to dictate what should be written in the opening. These ideas are scribed on the chalkboard, overhead projector, or chart paper. As the writing unfolds, students offer revisions for what has been written. These responses are considered, and revisions are made when agreed to by the class.

(5) Following the drafting of the introduction, the first similarity or difference is selected and addressed. Once again, various students dictate their ideas, and these ideas are recorded by the teacher. Critiques of the ideas written are encouraged and revisions are initiated when and where appropriate.
(6) The shared writing continues until all similarities and differences are addressed, or until the teacher believes that the students have developed an understanding of the process.
(7) After reviewing the purpose of a conclusion, the students dictate one for their compare-and-contrast text.

Choral Writing

In deconstructing the scaffold and having learners assume more responsibility, choral writing requires student to generate both meaning and written language itself. Once again using a chalkboard, overhead projector, or chart paper, the teacher and students collaboratively generate and scribe a written text. Different students come to the chalkboard, overhead projector, or chart paper and individually write a portion of the text. At times, the teacher also records his or her ideas as well. In choral writing, in contrast to shared writing, students take on the added responsibility of physically putting their ideas on the page.

The choral writing of the compare-and-contrast text might reflect the following features:

(1) After students have read several texts that address the topic under consideration in different ways, the teacher constructs a 3-column T-chart on the chalkboard, overhead projector, or chart paper. Individual students come forward and record a similarity or difference found in the readings. The teacher also adds to the T-chart when appropriate.
(2) Once a substantial number of similarities and differences have been identified and recorded, the students decide which ones are to be addressed, and their order.
(3) After a brief discussion in which students review the purpose of an introduction, students brainstorm what information is to be included in the introduction. Individual students take turns to write the introduction on the chalk-board, overhead projector, or chart paper. As with all steps in this process, what has been written is evaluated and revised as necessary.
(4) Following the introduction, individual students take turns to write about one similarity or difference.
(5) Once again, the purpose of a conclusion is reviewed, ideas are brainstormed, and a conclusion drafted.

Guided Writing

In guided writing, students individually engage in the writing process, with the teacher providing support and direction as required. The primary responsibility for writing belongs to that of the individual student, with the teaching acting as a 'guide at the side.' This contrasts with choral writing, in which the text evolved through the efforts of the group and no one student was responsible for the text in its entirety.

At this point in the writing of the compare-and-contrast text, the teacher's responsibility has significantly lessened:

(1)   The teacher introduces to the students the topic to be compared and contrasted.

(2)   Students individually write their own texts. During this writing, the teacher circulates around the room providing assistance. At times, if several students are experiencing the same difficulty, a small group might be formed and the teacher provides instruction to help students solve the problem.

Paired Writing

In paired writing, responsibility for mediation continues to shift from the teacher to the students. Students are paired to collaboratively and largely independently write a text. In pairing the students, the teacher should consider personality and ability. Obviously, students' personalities and temperaments should be compatible. Additionally, each student should have sufficient linguistic and cognitive abilities to contribute to the collaboration.

The teacher's primary responsibility at this point in the writing process is to:

(1)   Introduce the topic to be compared and contrasted, and to identify the writing partners.

(2)   As the students write, the teacher must be available for assistance. However, in contrast to guided writing, the pairs should largely be able to write the text independently.

Independent Writing

Independent writing activities are those that individual students are able to accomplish on their own. The teacher may be available for assistance but, for the most part, students should be writing on their own.

The previous sequence of mediational structures can be modified in various ways so as to provide the necessary support for the English language learners being taught. Modifications should be based on the needs of the students as well as on the demands of the writing event that is being introduced to the students. If the writing makes few linguistic and cognitive demands on the students, the teacher provides less instructional support. When demands are great, teacher support will also need to be great. The power of this mediational framework is that it is not writing-task specific. Any writing in which the teacher wishes the students to engage can be structured using this framework.

It is also important to keep in mind that the writing process is never mastered. There will always be writing activities that place linguistic and cognitive demands on students that will cause difficulties. Students, for example, may come to control the writing of compare-and-contrast texts, but may still struggle when they are asked to analyze and synthesize information from multiple sources. This means that the degree of mediation will continue to vary as students experience a wealth of writing experiences in the upper elementary grades.

WRITING IN THE DISCIPLINES: MOVING BEYOND PERSONAL EXPERIENCES AND NARRATIVES

As we saw in Chapter 3, in the upper elementary grades students are frequently introduced to new text structures in new disciplines. Many students, bilingual or monolingual, find writing in the disciplines to be challenging. Typically, in the earlier elementary grades they would not have had experience with disciplinary-based writing and would have focused on the reporting of facts and figures in their writing. However, writing in the disciplines involves more than the reporting of information. It also involves an understanding of the various forms of knowledge within the content areas. Students must also be helped to think about and manipulate this knowledge in various ways through the process of writing. Various text structures exist to help students accomplish this goal: time order, compare and contrast, problem and solution, cause and effect, and idea development. Figure 4.2 represents the organization of these structures. We will shortly demonstrate how these structures can be used to help ELLs visually understand the overall arrangement of meanings within each structure.

As illustrated in Figure 4.2, time-order texts typically contain a setting and at least one episode. Within the episode, there is an initiating event or action that serves to cause an internal response or goal in the main character. This goal causes an action on the part of the character in an attempt to obtain the goal. The consequence marks the character's attainment or non-attainment of the goal. Finally, the reaction expresses the main character's feeling about attaining or not attaining the goal. For most ELLs, this is the structure with which they are most familiar and comfortable.

Compare-and-contrast texts address the ways in which ideas, issues, or events are similar and different. Problem-and-solution texts present a problem with a number of possible solutions, or several problems that can be resolved by a single solution. Cause-and effect structures demonstrate how particular events occur or come into being (effect) because of other events (cause). Finally, texts that focus on idea development are structured by the presentation of facts, concepts, and generalizations. Frequently, facts are organized and related to concepts, and concepts are organized and related to generalizations. The order in which facts, concepts, and generalizations are presented is usually determined by importance or significance.

It is important to be mindful of the fact, however, that texts may actually contain a

- **Time order**

  Setting + episode [initiating event + internal response + attempt + consequence + reaction]

- **Compare and contrast**

- **Problem and solution**

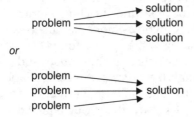

or

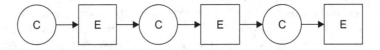

- **Cause and effect**

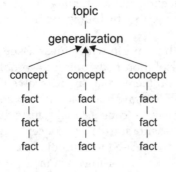

Figure 4.2 Text structures and the writing process

mix of these structures, and students should be helped to understand this fact. Informational texts that focus on the development of ideas, commonly found in the social sciences, may include the kind of time-sequenced events that typically are found in literary narratives. Similarly, problem-and-solution structured science texts may in many ways resemble the structure of -ordered ideas in a literary novel.

When teachers introduce the various cognitive and linguistic frameworks to their students, it is important to consider how knowledge is manipulated and how it is expressed in writing. These frameworks need to be embedded within contexts that require their use. Too often, students are taught to write in the various structures without first considering why a particular structure is necessary. That is, the purpose or function of the text within the communicative context is not examined. Rather, students simply learn the patterns and structures, and demonstrate their knowledge when required, such as on standardized tests. If students are to be helped to use various literacy forms in the 'real world,' a consideration of their appropriate use in various contexts must be an essential part of instruction (Kucer, 2001).

Not only do English language learners need to be taught these various thinking and text structures, they also need to be taught the language that is used to express them. Commonly referred to as signals or connectives, this language expresses the conceptual relationship that the writer is wanting to convey. It is the writer's way of signaling to the reader that a particular connection of ideas is being represented. Table 4.2 lists groups of connective or signal words and the relationships they express. As might be expected, some text structures make use of particular relationships more often than others. For example, as illustrated in Table 4.3, time-order texts frequently employ such words as 'not long after,' 'as', 'before,' and 'when.' Problem–and-solution structured texts make use of 'because,' 'therefore,' 'consequently,' etc.

Most English language learners will need to be explicitly taught many of the text structures and the corresponding language expressions. Keeping in mind the mediational framework previously delineated, we have found that reading is one of the best places to begin to develop this conceptual and linguistic knowledge.

HELPING STUDENTS ORGANIZE TEXT STRUCTURES

In many of the disciplines, the exploration of problems and solutions is a commonly found text structure. Students not only need to understand how these structures operate in reading, but how to produce them in their own writing. We will use the problem-and-solution structure to demonstrate how teachers can link reading to writing and help students develop an understanding of various text structures and their language. However, any text structure can be taught in a similar manner. We will also introduce the use of a second mediational framework (into, through, and beyond) to illustrate how students can be given the support required to become proficient with this or any text structure (Kucer *et al.*, 1995).

Table 4.2 Text signals and the writing process

Connectives/signals: A special type of word that indicate conceptual relationships among various ideas across the sentence or text.	
Connective/signal	*Indicated relationship*
also, again, another, finally, furthermore, likewise, moreover, similarly, too	another item in the same series
afterwards, finally, later, on, next, after	another item in a time series
for instance, for example, specifically	another example or illustration of what has been said
accordingly, as a result, consequently, hence, then, therefore, thus, so	a consequence of what has been said
in other words, that is to say, to put it differently	a restatement of what has been said
all in all, altogether, finally, in conclusion, the point is	a concluding item or summary
but, however, on the other hand, on the contrary	a statement opposing what has been said
granted, of course, to be sure, undoubtedly	a concession to an opposing view
all the same, even though, nevertheless, nonetheless, still	the original line of argument is resuming after a concession

Table 4.3 Text structures, signals, and the writing process

Text structure	*Typical connective/signal*
Time order	time, not long after, now, as, before, after, when
Compare and contrast	however, but, as well as, on the other hand, not only ... but also, either ... or, while, although, unless, similarly, yet
Problem and solution	because, since, therefore, so that, consequently, as a result, this led
Cause and effect	to, so that, nevertheless, thus, accordingly, if ... then
Idea development	begin with, first, secondly, next, finally, most important, also, in fact, for instance, for example

Into Strategies

Into strategies are those instructional actions that prepare students for engagement with a particular activity. In this case, it is those strategies with which students are engaged before writing a problem-and-solution text. Since in many cases English language learners at the upper elementary level are more proficient in reading than in writing, and because written discourse can demonstrate to students the features of problem-and-solution texts, the use of reading will permeate these 'into strategies.'

(1)   Locate several well-structured problem-and-solution texts. If this structure is to be used in a writing activity from a particular discipline, the texts should come from that discipline. It is also advisable that these texts are fairly short in nature so that the overall problem-and-solution structure is readily apparent and can be easily discovered by the students.

(2)   Ask students to read one of the texts selected. The kind of support provided for this reading will vary, depending on the ability of the students; you may engage the students in shared reading, paired reading, independent reading, etc.

(3)   Share with the students a road map of a particular geographical location. Ask the students what purposes road maps can serve. In this discussion, highlight the notion that maps of this nature typically represent significant locations and significant routes from one place to another.

(4)   Discuss with the students that all texts have a general organizational pattern, similar to that of a road map. In a text structure, however, what is represented are major ideas and how they connect to one another.

(5)   On a chalkboard, overhead projector, or chart paper, show the students the appropriate problem-and-solution framework illustrated in Figure 4.2. With the class, identify the problem(s) and solutions(s) in the text that was read, and list them on the framework.

(6)   On a chalkboard, overhead projector, or chart paper, show the text that the student read. Underline all the connective or signal words in the text. Ask the students what each underlined word means or does in the text and why the author selected that word to use.

(7)   As each word is discussed, list the word and the relationship indicated on a wall chart for future use and reference, similar to that shown in Table 4.2.

(8)   Give students the opportunity to read additional problem-and-solution tests. You can mediate this learning by adapting the framework for writing previously addressed in Table 4.1 and applying it to the reading of problem-and-solution texts. Before moving to 'through' strategies, students should have a fairly clear understanding of the organizational pattern of problem and solution texts.

Through Strategies

'Through' strategies are those support systems that guide students as they actually engage with the activity. For the writing of a problem-and-solution text, they are the strategies that guide students as they write:

(1)   Once students have an understanding of the problem-and-solution structure from their reading, they are ready to apply this understanding to their writing. Based on content that the students have been studying, problems are identified and discussed. On a chalkboard, overhead projector, or chart paper, the teacher records the problems.
(2)   As a whole class, in small groups, or individually, depending on the needs of the students, possible solutions are identified, listed, and discussed for each problem, similar to that shown in Figure 4.2.
(3)   Using the problems and solutions identified, the students select a problem(s)-and-solution(s) structure to write about, and draw the structure. Each student must either have one problem with several possible solutions, or several problems with one solution.
(4)   Using their structure as a guide, students write problem-and-solution texts.

Beyond Strategies

'Beyond' strategies help students to reflect on what they have accomplished and learned. Beyond strategies bring to conscious awareness the processes in which students have engaged:

(1)   After students have drafted their problem-and-solution texts, they share their texts in a small group or with a partner.
(2)   As each text is shared, students identify the problem and solution.
(3)   Students also identify signals or connectives that have been used in the text. If additional signals or connectives are warranted, these are suggested and discussed.

HELPING STUDENTS ORGANIZE TEXT MEANINGS

Not only do writers use existing text structures to order their ideas, they also consider what ideas need to be addressed. A significant part of the writing process involves generating and organizing major ideas. As writers put pen to paper, they continually seek to discover their major ideas and how the ideas relate to one another. Frequently, because the previous instructional focus has been on writing conventions (e.g. spelling, punctuation, capitalization, sentence syntax), many upper elementary ELLs students fail to consider what ideas need to be expressed. They are so concerned with the surface structure of the text that they ignore meaning. The following strategy lesson helps ELL students to rediscover the meaning base of all acts of writing (Kucer, 1986; Kucer & Silva, in progress).

Into Strategies

(1)   Inform the students that they are going to be doing some writing. This writing may be on an assigned topic related to a theme under study or students may select their own topic. If necessary, brainstorm possible writing topics with the students, and record them on the board.

(2)   Give the students several cards and ask them to write down several things they might write about. If the teacher has specified a general topic, students can generate specific subtopics related to the general topic.

(3)   As the generating of topics is taking place, the ideas should be informally shared, allowing for further stimulation of possible writing topics.

(4)   Once adequate time for generating and sharing has been allowed, the students are to select the topic card on which they would most like to write. All other cards are put into student 'writing topics' envelopes that can be used at some other time.

Through Strategies

(1)   After selecting their topics, the students must think of all of the major or big ideas that are related to their topic. These major ideas are also recorded on individual cards, one idea per card. The students should be encouraged to generate as many major-idea cards as possible – more than they might be able to actually use. This brainstorming process will open the students to the possibility of discovering new ideas. Because the language on the cards simply serves as a placeholder for meaning, its length should not be restricted or specified.

(2)   As was done with the topic cards, give students the opportunity to share their major ideas.

(3)   After time has been allowed for generating and sharing major-idea cards, the students must select those cards they predict will be included in their texts. Cards not used should be set aside. The cards chosen should then be laid across a table or desk and put in the order that the students predict they will appear in their texts.

(4)   In small groups, students should briefly discuss their ideas cards and explain the reasons why the cards are arranged as they are.

(5)   At this point in the activity, using the cards as a guide, the writing of the texts begins. Because the cards are only placeholders for predicted meanings, the writers are free to accept or reject these predictions in any way they choose. Cards may be taken out, added, or reordered as required. The teacher should not expect to find a one-to-one correspondence between the cards and the actual text produced.

Beyond Strategies

(1)   After the drafts have been completed, give students the opportunity to share what they have written.
(2)   If the texts are to be published, engage the students in writing conferences, and provide time for revision and editing.

This strategy can also be used to support upper elementary ELLs as they write research papers using multiple sources. Many students experience difficulty integrating and synthesizing information. Too often, these papers are simply 'retellings' of what has been read. After students have recorded notes on the topic under investigation, ask them to review their notes, looking for the major ideas to include in their papers. Students write each major idea on a three-by-five card, and the cards are then arranged in a meaningful order. Students use their cards as a guide when they write their reports. To help students move away from 'copying' their notes, they may be told that they must first review their notes corresponding to their first card. Then, without referring back to their notes, they must write about their first major idea. They then review their notes related to the second card, put their notes aside, and write about the second card. This procedure continues until all the cards have been written about. After drafts have been completed, students can then return to their notes to expand what has been written.

CONCLUSION

This chapter has focused on supporting English language learners in their development of various text structures as well as text meanings. This developmental support focused on ways in which scaffolds could be constructed and deconstructed over time so as to support students in taking on increased responsibility in the writing process, especially writing within the disciplines. Although specific strategy lessons were explored, the teacher will want to take the mediational frameworks presented and apply them to whatever types of writing happens to be relevant within his or her classroom.

Instructional Practices to Promote Reading Development in English Language Learners

Introduction

Instructional Frameworks to Scaffold
ELLs' Reading Development

Making Use of Reading Strategies to
Construct Meaning

Instructional Strategies to Facilitate
ELLs' Construction of Meaning

Questioning that Supports
Comprehension

Conclusion

CHAPTER 5

Instructional Practices to Promote Reading Development in English Language Learners

INTRODUCTION

Reading is a process in which readers, using their linguistic knowledge and experiential background, construct meaning from the printed text. This interaction between the reader and the text as the reader constructs meaning is a social and communicative act. In the social context of the classroom, students move to new levels of literacy learning through contact with the teacher and other students. In addition, literacy learning is enhanced as students engage in independent literacy activities and home-related academic experiences.

While there is wide national debate as to how best to provide literacy instruction in the primary grades, the issue of how to address the literacy instructional needs of upper elementary students has received far less attention. This is problematic because the upper elementary grades present a unique set of literacy challenges for students. As was discussed in Chapter 4, these challenges are in the form of what students are expected to do and also in the amount of support and mediation that is available to them. In some schools, the amount of time in which students are 'learning to read' is significantly reduced. At the same time, there is considerably more need for students to 'read to learn' as they encounter complex content area texts. This period is also marked by a greater emphasis on reading nonfiction texts that are longer in length and more complicated than the narrative texts read in the earlier grades.

If this situation is problematic for the general school population, it is even more so for English language learners (ELLs), who enter the upper elementary grades faced with a marked increase in the challenges presented by literacy tasks. For ELLs, whose prior knowledge often does not match what the school expects, the task of constructing meaning from text is made more difficult as readers meet increasing numbers of words that are not in their listening vocabularies. In addition, these students are faced with greater and greater cognitive demands as they are expected to make use of a wide range of word identification and comprehension skills and strategies. As a result of the burden that literacy tasks in the upper elementary grades place on these students, many ELLs lose their motivation and interest in reading.

This chapter describes instructional frameworks that can scaffold or support the reading development of ELLs. These reading mediational frameworks parallel those described for writing in the previous chapter with a focus on their instructional efficacy for ELLs. The second part of the chapter addresses some specific reading and instructional strategies that are designed to facilitate ELLs' abilities to meet the increased reading demands of the upper elementary classroom. Although these strategies are also appropriate for monolingual students, our focus in this chapter is how these strategies might be adapted for ELLs. As discussed in Chapter 4, we understand that time and workload constraints make it difficult for most teachers to provide separate and unique assignments for the ELL student. However, we believe that adopting the strategies and activities described is within teachers' means to accomplish and will often help struggling monolingual students as well. Finally, we will focus on an asset that bilinguals bring to the reading process, their knowledge of another language.

INSTRUCTIONAL FRAMEWORKS TO SCAFFOLD ENGLISH LANGUAGE LEARNERS' READING DEVELOPMENT

Reading, like writing (see Chapter 4), is a process in which students move from their potential to their actual independent reading abilities (Kucer, 2001). As educators, it is our goal to support students as they develop into competent and independent readers. To do this, it is necessary to use reading instructional frameworks that provide varying degrees of scaffolding for ELLs according to their needs. As with writing, there are different types of reading instruction (Cooper with Kiger, 2003), and teachers determine the 'best match' for students based on their cognitive and reading abilities, the particular piece of written text to be read, and the lesson's focus or purpose. Knowing the different instructional options provides teachers with a good resource in their efforts to help ELLs become successful readers. Five reading instructional frameworks are listed below with an explanation of how they can be adapted in helping ELL students to develop literacy competency. These frameworks are: reading aloud, shared reading, guided reading, paired reading, and independent reading.

Reading Aloud

In 'reading aloud,' the teacher or other fluent reader reads a piece of literature to the students, either as a large group or in small groups. As an instructional framework, reading aloud provides the opportunity to expose students to text that they might be unable to read on their own because of difficult vocabulary and/or complex concepts. While reading the selection aloud, the teacher models fluent reading and the use of reading strategies that facilitate comprehension. This mode is especially recommended for ELLs, many of whom need to 'hear' how fluent English reading sounds. These students can benefit greatly from listening to the intonation, phrasing and pronunciation of English words, and other features of oral reading as modeled by the teacher. In reading-aloud sessions, the students listen to the teacher read without seeing the text. As they listen, they are encouraged to enjoy and appreciate the selection. Both short selections that can be completed in a single reading, and chapter books that will be read over several sessions are appropriate for reading aloud. While it is sometimes thought that reading to students is an instructional practice that is primarily geared to the early childhood classes, it is actually suitable for all grade levels.

For ELLs in the upper elementary grades, reading aloud offers many opportunities to scaffold or support students' reading. Before reading the selection, questions can be asked to elicit information that will help students to connect their experiences with the literature. For example, before reading, *How Many Days to America? A Thanksgiving Story* (Bunting, 1988), students can be asked to think about their own experiences in coming to the United States and their feelings about leaving their native land. In the pre-reading part of the reading-aloud lesson, students can also be guided to use the title of the selection as the basis for making predictions about the contents of the reading. Also, as students become more aware of a particular author's style, attention can be drawn to the author as well as to additional texts by the same author. For ELLs, who may not be familiar with these and other components of written English text, reading aloud can offer a number of instructional opportunities. For example, lessons can be built around exploring the organizational features of a book, such as copyright, publisher's information, and table of contents.

During the reading of the selection, the teacher stops reading at pre-determined points and with the students reviews the events or information that has been read. This is also a time to elicit predictions from the students about what they think will happen in the next section of the reading. Since ELLs often need additional linguistic and conceptual support in English, this can be a time to clarify confusing concepts and present vocabulary in context.

After reading, students can be asked to check their initial predictions. Students can then become involved in making a personal response to the reading. This response may be made in any one of a variety of forms, such as journal writing, art projects, or dramatizations. For example, after reading, *Felita* (Mohr, 1979), a story that describes the experiences of a Puerto Rican girl as she moves out of her familiar New York neighborhood to another 'better' neighborhood, one way that students can respond is by writing in double-entry journals. In a double-entry journal, the page is divided into two columns. In the left column, students can chose and write direct quotes from the book, and they then use the right column to record their reflections on each quote. The reflection may be in the form of a reaction to the quote, a question generated by the quote, or any other connection the student wishes to make. Other responses may be in the form of fine arts or drama, either of which is a natural partner to literature. Both art and drama could be used in a post-reading response to *Sarah, Plain and Tall* (MacLachlan, 1985), a story that chronicles the arrival of Sarah Wheaton, a mail-order bride from Maine, who has travelled to the prairies of the Midwest to become part of the Witting family. An art-related project might involve the reader drawing a story character, cutting it out, and mounting it on a strip of heavy paper (which will also serve as a stand for the cut-out). Along the strip, the reader writes one or more sentences describing the traits of the character. Likewise, any of the chapters in *Sarah, Plain and Tall* lend themselves to dramatization. The chapter can either be rewritten as a script or read in its original form with the students taking on the roles of the respective characters.

Although the reading-aloud type of instruction is recommended for all students, the following steps are suggested for reading aloud to ELLs (Ruddell, 2002):

(1) Choose a piece of literature that you want to read aloud, preferably one that taps into ELLs' interests or cultural background
(2) Elicit a positive stance toward the content of the selection and, if reading a narrative, help students to identify with the key characters. Encourage students to listen in order to enjoy and appreciate the text.
(3) Become familiar with the text and think about the moods and feelings you wish to convey. Practice reading orally so that you are prepared to deliver the proper intonation and timing.
(4) Before reading the selection, identify the background information and new concepts that may need to be explained. Decide how you will want the students to respond after the reading.
(5) Arrange the physical setting of the classroom to provide a comfortable atmo-sphere for listening to the reading.
(6) Read the selection, modulating your voice as appropriate to help students to visualize the characters, setting, mood, and the plot development if you are reading a story. Use visual aids as well. Use question prompts that focus on the gist of a story or the main points of informational text. If reading a chapter book, encourage students to summarize what has already been read and to make predictions about the next section to be read.
(7) Allow sufficient time for responses.

We are also reminded to expect minor distractions when reading aloud. Particu-larly with ELLs (who may be influenced by a native cultural tradition that calls for a choral response to the spoken word), students may spontaneously comment aloud or whisper to a neighbor about the story events or content of the reading. These behaviors are a form of reader response, and responding is to be encouraged as it is a sign of enjoyment.

When the genre of the read aloud is a story, the Directed-Reading-Listening-Thinking Activity (DRLTA) is a procedure that has been used successfully with

ELLs (Diamond & Moore, 1995). During the DRLTA, students listen and make predictions and inferences as the teacher reads the story. The listening and predicting continue throughout the story reading, with the teacher stopping at the pre-determined points so that students can check their predictions. This strategy works both with long readings (e.g. chapter books) and with shorter texts (e.g. short stories). The steps involved in implementing DRLTA include:

(1) Assess the prior knowledge that students will need to understand the text. Provide background knowledge where necessary.
(2) Show the book, calling attention to the title and any accompanying illustrations.
(3) Ask questions that will elicit predictions and set a purpose for reading. For example, looking at the title of the book, ask 'What do you think this story will be about?' 'What do you think we will find out as we read?'
(4) Read to the pre-determined stop points asking questions as you go along. For example, ask 'Now what do you think will happen next?' 'Why do you think so?' 'Are there any clues that support your prediction?' 'How would you feel if (ask students to put themselves in a character's place) that happened to you?'

When using the reading-aloud framework with ELLs, Diamond and Moore (1995) also recommend the Story Grammar Reading Thinking Activity (SGRTA). In SGTRA, the elements of story grammar (characters, setting, goals or problems, actions or events, and resolutions) form the basis for supporting students' understanding of the story. The steps for implementing SGRTA are similar to DRLTA:

(1) Build background knowledge.
(2) Introduce the story.
(3) Read the story to the students, pausing to ask questions, then continuing to read. Base your questions on story grammar.
(4) Work with students to create a story map as story is read.

Shared Reading

Based on the shared-book experience (Holdaway, 1979), this procedure was originally developed for beginning readers. It can be adapted for use with students who are not able to read the text in literary works, trade books, or content books on their own. In shared reading, students follow along in their own books, on an overhead transparency, or a big book as the teacher reads the text aloud. In subsequent readings, students may either join in the reading together with the teacher or may 'chime in' at designated points (Freeman & Freeman, 2002). Shared Reading is especially suited for ELLs because, like Reading Aloud, it provides a model of fluent English oral reading and utilizes similar procedures for scaffolding understanding before, during, and after reading.

Shared reading is especially suited for helping ELLs to develop reading fluency through choral reading. This is because a factor that often inhibits ELLs' ability to actively engage in classroom tasks is anxiety over their lack of English proficiency

(Pappamihiel, 2002). An ELL in the upper elementary grades, who is lacking in English oral reading fluency, tends to feel anxious if asked to read orally as an individual, but is comfortable when reading in chorus. Although poems are most often used for choral reading, other texts such as plays with chorus parts can also lend themselves to this format to build fluency.

Shared reading also offers students the opportunity to use oral reading to express the meaning of the literary piece. For example, after modeling the oral reading of the text, the teacher invites the students to reread the passage orally together. ELLs can be encouraged to use their voices to show their interpretation of the meanings and the feelings that the passage evokes in them. Using choral reading in this way offers students the opportunity to focus on how they as readers are experiencing the literary piece. This is called aesthetic reading, and the primary focus of readers' attention is centered directly on what they are living through during their relationship with that particular text (Rosenblatt, 1978).

Tompkins (2001) suggests four possible arrangements for choral reading of poetry; they can all be adapted for use with prose:

(1) **Echo reading:** in this arrangement students repeat each line after the teacher or lead reader.
(2) **Leader and chorus reading:** the poem is divided, with the leader reading the main parts and the students reading the refrain or chorus in unison.
(3) **Small-group reading:** after dividing into groups, each group of students reads a part of the poem.
(4) **Cumulative reading:** in this arrangement, one student or group reads the first line or stanza of the poem and another student or group joins in at each line or stanza, creating a cumulative effect, as in the following example:

Student 1:	*'T was the night before Christmas*
Students 1 and 2:	*When all through the house*
Students 1, 2, and 3:	*Not a creature was stirring*
Students 1, 2, 3, and 4:	*Not even a mouse.*

(from *A Visit from St Nicholas or T'was the Night Before Christmas*, Clement C. Moore, 1985)

Guided Reading

Guided reading is an instructional framework that is designed to help students become competent readers who can 'process increasingly challenging texts with understanding and fluency' (Fountas & Pinnell, 2001: 193). Although there are some variations in how guided reading is implemented, basically, it is used as a means to scaffold instruction while students construct meaning from text. In guided reading, teachers are able to monitor and provide support for students as they apply reading skills and strategies during reading. Given the strong emphasis on monitoring and support built into the guided reading format, it is particularly suitable for ELLs.

Guided reading works most effectively when teachers meet with small groups of students who are at the same level of reading proficiency. Since guided reading requires more independent reading on the part of the student than either reading aloud or shared reading, text material should be somewhat challenging, but it is recommended that students should be able to read approximately 95% of the words. However, with ELLs, many of whom are older learners, it is essential that the text content is age appropriate.

In preparing and teaching a guided reading lesson, we recommend that teachers follow these steps:

(1) Analyze the text to identify difficult vocabulary and complex concepts for which you may need to provide supportive instruction prior to reading. As an example, ELLs might find the use of figurative language (such as metaphors) in a selection difficult to understand.
(2) Introduce the book. This will involve activating students' prior knowledge, providing background where needed, eliciting predictions, and helping students to connect their background experience to the reading.
(3) Instruct students to read the previously designated sections/chapter silently.
(4) Revisit predictions after reading. Ask: 'Were our predictions confirmed?' 'How did our predictions match up with what we read?'
(5) Continue the discussion, helping to clarify students' understanding as needed.
(6) Teach a mini-lesson that focuses on a skill/strategy found in the text (for example, understanding the use of metaphors to make comparisons).
(7) Engage students in extension activities in which they can respond to the selection. Some possible activities can include journal writing, drawing, and dramatizations.

Paired Reading

In paired reading, students read or reread a literary selection with each other – students are often able to read a selection together that they would not be able to read independently (Cooper with Kiger, 2003). For ELLs, paired reading offers the opportunity for social interaction as they enjoy the reading together with peers. As was stated in Chapter 4, this social support can facilitate the ELLs' movement from their potential abilities to the development of new literacy competency.

Independent Reading

In independent reading, students read a text, which they often chose themselves. As an instructional framework, independent reading can be coupled with class-room organizational structures such as literature circles or a reading workshop. Independent reading in this context differs from the voluntary independent reading that students do throughout the day or at home, and which is not usually used as a means of reading instruction. As an instructional framework, independent reading provides the least amount of scaffolding and so the texts to be used should either be written at a level that the student can read independently or should be texts that have already been read, and with teacher support can be reread. ELLs often have limited opportunities to receive instruction via independent reading. This is because they are perceived as 'at risk' readers (Allington & Walmsley, 1995). It is essential that all students, including ELLs, have opportunities to experience instruction through independent reading regardless of their level of reading ability.

When reading independently, students can respond either individually (e.g. through a journal entry) or as a member of a group. Cooper with Kiger (2003) suggest the following variation of the literature-circle format as a guide for the group literature discussion.

(1)   The student tells the title and author of the book.
(2)   The student talks about his/her book. Some suggested prompts include:
   •   talking about the reader's favorite part;
   •   relating the book to the reader's own life experiences;
   •   identifying techniques used by the author that lead the reader to have strong feelings about a particular character;
   •   commenting on events that have occurred in the story since the previous group discussion;
   •   predicting what will happen next.

MAKING USE OF READING STRATEGIES TO CONSTRUCT MEANING

As we have been discussing, reading is a dynamic process in which the reader constructs meaning through interacting with the text. Meaning is constructed and changed as the reader's prior knowledge, the text, and the reading context or situation interact. In addition, research has shown that good readers, in contrast to poor readers, use strategies before, during, and after reading in order to facilitate this meaning-making process. The good news for us is that, although struggling readers may not use strategies efficiently, they can be taught to do so and thus improve their comprehension skills.

The question for us then becomes what are the best strategies for our students to use in order to increase their ability to construct meaning from text? In reviewing the research on the use of reading strategies, Cooper with Kiger (2003) identified some of the strategies that are considered important for reading success:

   •   visualizing;
   •   monitoring;
   •   inferring and predicting;
   •   identifying important information;
   •   generating and answering questions;
   •   summarizing.

In the following section, we will describe each of the these reading strategies and offer suggestions as to how they might be incorporated into literacy instruction for upper elementary struggling readers.

Visualizing

Visualizing involves making pictures in our heads as we read. Through visualizing what is written in the text, the reader engages in inferential thinking that actually expands the textual information provided. For example, if we were to read a story set in a restaurant, our experience and prior knowledge of eating in restaurants would allow us to create a mental image of the scene and add details that are not provided in the written text. This additional information serves to increase our understanding, and facilitates our meaning-construction process.

A key to using visualization, as shown in the restaurant example, is reliance on prior knowledge. This prior knowledge refers not only to past experience with the text content (e.g. eating in a restaurant) but also to other elements of the text, such as genre. Also, as we read further in the text, we often need to adjust our visualizations as we gain more information. In working with ELLs, the issue of prior knowledge is significant. As we teach ELLs to engage in the strategic use of visualization, we need to make sure that they have the necessary prior knowledge to do so. Dramatization is also a means of fostering visualization as students are asked to picture what the scene to be acted out might look like.

To help students make strategic use of visualization, teachers can remind them to 'make pictures' in their heads while reading the words. For ELLs, who benefit from the added support of a visual cue, this reminder can be posted on a chart and displayed in the classroom.

Vocabulary development, a crucial area in ELLs' literacy achievement, can be enhanced through visualization. In the Key Word Approach (Gunning, 2000), as an aid to remembering words, students are taught through images to associate a meaning with a key word. For example, for the word *antique*, the key word may be 'ant' and the student makes a mental picture of an *ant* sitting in a rocking chair. The student is encouraged to visualize the picture as vividly as possible. The *ant* may have a gray beard and there may be a cane resting near the rocking chair. This image of an 'elderly ant' serves as a connection between the word, *antique* and its meaning. With some words it is not possible for the key word to be a whole word in its own right; instead, the key word be just the beginning letters. As an example, the word, *pet* could be the key word for *pelican*, and the mental picture could be of a person holding a pet pelican.

When using this approach with ELLs, the teacher may need to create the image for the students. In the following scenario, Mr Wilson, a fourth- grade teacher, used this technique to help the ELLs in his class learn and remember the word *mandolin*.

Scenario: Visualizing the Word 'mandolin'

Mr Wilson writes the word, **mandolin**, on the board and explains that it is a type of stringed musical instrument. He accompanies this explanation with a picture of a mandolin. He then helps the students to choose the word **man** as the key word for *mandolin*. Mr Wilson asks the students to visualize a picture of a man playing the stringed instrument, the mandolin. He asks individual students to illustrate their visualizations on chart paper. Mr Wilson does this to help those ELLs who may be having difficulty conjuring up their own mental images. When he feels satisfied that all the students have been able to create mental images to link mandolin with its meaning, Mr Wilson reminds the students that when they see the word in the future, they should recall the pictures they have made 'in their heads'.

Monitoring

Monitoring is a process that involves the reader's awareness that there is a comprehension difficulty, that the text is not 'making sense' and having a strategy for fixing the difficulty. It is the major component of metacognitive development (Baker & Brown, 1984). Monitoring is developmental in nature and increases as the reader matures. Some of the behaviors that readers engage in to monitor their comprehension include: rereading, reading ahead, revising predictions and making new ones, questioning, evaluating the text, using word identification strategies, looking up words, and asking for outside help. Frequently, ELLs need explicit instruction in monitoring their reading, particularly since they may be unaware of a comprehension breakdown because of their lack of sophisticated vocabulary and syntactical knowledge in English. Modeling by the teacher or by a more proficient peer can be an effective means for helping ELLs to develop monitoring abilities. Table 5.1 lists some questions that ELLs might be taught to ask themselves as they read in order to monitor their meaning construction.

Table 5.1 Think and check

You can check your understanding as you read.
THINK:

(1) Is this selection making sense?

(2) If I'm having trouble understanding, I can:
     read the selection again;
     keep on reading to see if it helps my understanding;
     look up words that are giving me trouble;
     ask for help.

Table 5.2 Making inferences

To make inferences as you read, ask yourself:

(1) Is the author giving me any clues in the text?

(2) What do I already know about the topic?

(3) If I put the author's clues and what I already know about the topic together, can I figure out what the author means?

Making Inferences and Predicting

Making inferences is the process of making educated guesses(Goodman, 1967), connections, and judgments about information that is not directly stated in the text. Making predictions about the information contained in text content before and during reading is also a form of inferring. To make inferences and predictions, readers have to rely on the available text information and on their own prior knowledge. As with visualizing, the key role of prior knowledge here means that we may have to provide additional background for ELLs to enable them to engage in inferring and predicting. Table 5.2 provides some questions to guide students in the use of this strategy.

Identifying Important Information

The ability to identify what is important information in a text is an essential factor that influences how the reader constructs meaning. Knowledge of text structure can be a useful tool in identifying the key points in a selection. Thus, when reading narrative text, knowledge of story grammar can help readers recognize the important components of that genre. Since we are particularly interested in struggling upper-elementary-grade ELL readers, it is important to note that, for this group we must be sure that the students have an understanding of what story grammar is, and what its individual components are. Sometimes, because such material has been presented in great detail in an earlier grade, there is a presumption that ELLs have internalized these understandings. However, because of their insufficiently developed proficiency in academic English, these understandings may not be in place for these students. Consequently, we must first provide these ELLs with direct instruction using many visuals that can aid them to understand what we mean by the terms: setting, characters, plot events, problem, climax, solution/resolution, etc. When this understanding is in place, then the strategy can be developed through teacher and/or peer modeling, possibly using a graphic such as a story map. Figures 5.1 and 5.2 provide examples of story maps.

Expository or informational text presents a particular challenge for ELLs, as this type of textual structure can be more difficult to recognize, and content materials often utilize more than one of these structures within a selection. While looking for

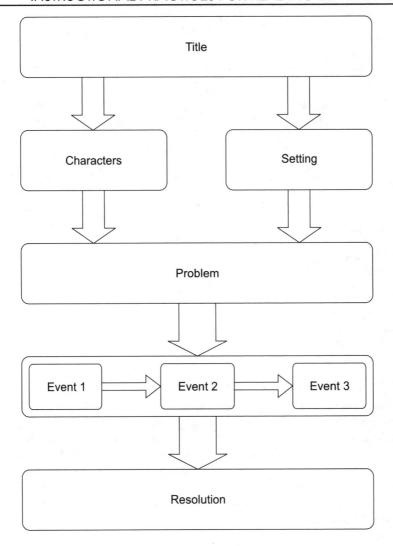

Figure 5.1 Story map 1

the signal words for a particular expository structure can be helpful here, a parallel instructional option is to teach the students to identify or infer the overall meaning or main idea of the passage. This ability to recognize the main idea of a passage is also necessary for summarizing, which is another strategy discussed in this chapter.

As with narrative text, instructional procedures such as modeling how to identify important textual information are also appropriate here. The points presented in Table 5.3 (Cooper with Kiger, 2003) can be used to help students identify important textual information.

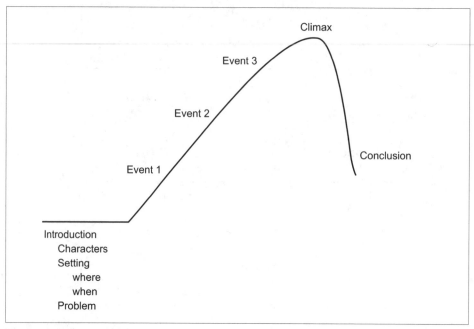

Figure 5.2 Story map 2

Generating and answering questions

Another important strategy that helps readers construct meaning before, during, and after reading is generating and answering questions. For this, we need to teach students how to formulate questions that will require them to engage in thinking and integrating information as they read (Cooper with Kiger, 2003). These may questions of a literal nature that can be answered with information found directly in the text, or they be ones that tap onto higher-level thinking and that require the reader either to make inferences or to make evaluations. They may also be a combination of all three types of questions.

Table 5.3 Reading informational text: Determining the important information

As you read, ask yourself:

(1) What is the topic of the selection? Looking to see what the information is mostly about will help you to determine what the topic is.

(2) Can you find a sentence that summarizes the paragraph/selection?

(3) Is there information in the selection that is not important to the topic?

(4) Based on what you have determined the important information to be, what do you think the main idea of the selection is?

Questioning in general has been found to be a valuable asset in promoting comprehension whether it is the reader, a peer, or the teacher who generates the questions. Reciprocal questioning, which will be discussed later in the chapter, makes extensive use of the question-generating strategy.

Summarizing

Considered by some to be the most effective reading strategy of all, summarizing is a process of stating in abbreviated form the essential ideas contained in a text. Summarizing is a strategy that is complex and, like other strategies we have discussed, must be explicitly taught to ELLs in general and to struggling ELL readers in particular. Presenting this strategy in its oral form as retelling is a good way to help students understand the concept of summarizing. Through the use of questioning, teachers can guide students to focus on the main ideas of the selection as they engage in retelling. Once students understand what it means to summarize, teachers can model how to compose written summaries of texts. Using content area texts (e.g. science, social studies), teachers can call students' attention to the end-of-chapter summaries. These content area texts can also be used for additional modeling of summarizing and to give students the opportunity for guided practice and independent application of this strategy. To provide ELLs with a guide to creating summaries, the following three steps are suggested (Gunning, 2000):

(1) Look at the title, headings, and beginning sentence to get the gist of what the topic and main idea might be. Also note the important details. Write either the main idea sentence from the text or, if there is none, compose one based on the topic information.
(2) Read the selection and write down any details that provide an explanation or description of the main idea.
(3) Read the summary. Eliminate any trivial details and combine details, where possible deleting any unnecessary words.

Although we still have more to learn about how readers use strategies, researchers and our own practical experience testify to the important place that strategy use holds in the profile of the successful ELL reader.

INSTRUCTIONAL STRATEGIES TO FACILITATE ENGLISH LANGUAGE LEARNERS' CONSTRUCTION OF MEANING

Helping ELLs to Activate and Develop Prior Knowledge

Prior knowledge is the information that comes out of an individual's background or previous experience (Harris & Hodges, 1995). It is universally agreed by authorities in the field of literacy that the prior knowledge that readers bring to the text plays an important role as they engage in the meaning-construction process. The role of prior knowledge is particularly significant for ELLs. ELLs come to school with culturally-based background knowledge that may differ from that of other mainstream students and from the expectations of the school. This 'mismatch' between students' background knowledge and what is needed to function success-fully in academic literacy tasks is a primary factor contributing to ELLs' level of achievement. For this reason, it is imperative that we pay special attention to ensuring that ELLs are supported in having access to the background required to engage in a particular reading task.

Among the kinds of prior knowledge that students must bring to the reading act are knowledge about the *textual structure* and knowledge about *textual content*. Both of these are necessary in helping the reader construct meaning. Strategies related to both *text structure* and *text content* are presented in the following sections.

Knowledge about Text Structures and Text Content

As students read, their understanding of the structure of the text facilitates their comprehension. Text structures may be divided into two major types: *narrative* and *expository*. Narrative text is found in stories and has a structural organization that includes a beginning, a middle, and an end of the story. Around this organizational structure may be built several story episodes comprising characters, setting, problem, goal, actions, and resolution/solution. These elements are called story grammar – a basic plan around which the story parts are interrelated. The use of graphic organizers such as story maps will help ELLs to understand the structure of narrative text and the elements of story grammar. Although organizers such as story maps are very helpful in familiarizing ELLs with the structure of narrative texts, most of the content material that students read in school is organized around expository text structures. Unlike narrative texts that are organized in clear-cut patterns, expository or informational structures are less clear, and are more difficult for students to read. This is especially true for ELLs, who may not be familiar with this style of written discourse commonly used in the United States and other English-speaking countries.

Knowledge about the content of the text is the second aspect of prior knowledge that we need to consider. Content knowledge includes important concepts and key vocabulary. While content knowledge can be addressed in narrative text, our focus here is content knowledge presented within the more difficult structures of expository text. Once students become aware of text structures, there are techniques that can help them organize expository text information graphically and see the relationships among concepts. Some of the text structures that students find in informational materials are:

- **Description**: this describes a topic by listing characteristics, details, and providing examples.
- **Sequence**: events are presented in chronological order. A parallel structure involves listing items in numerical order.

- **Compare–contrast**: the differences and similarities between two or more things are presented.
- **Problem–solution**: a problem is stated and one or more solutions offered.
- **Cause–effect**: the reader is presented with one or more causes followed by the effects.

Words that signal these structures in text, and suggested graphic organizers are presented in Table 5.4.

Strategies to Foster Independence in Activating Prior Knowledge

It is our goal as teachers to help our students become independent readers. To achieve this, students must be able to activate their prior knowledge independently. For ELLs, this involves having a means to organize their thinking in English. In the following section, we present some of the strategies that will foster this independence.

Anticipation Guide

In an anticipation guide, students indicate if they agree or disagree with debatable statements about the topic before the selection is read. This technique serves not only to activate prior knowledge but also builds interest and helps set a purpose for reading.

K-W-L Strategy

The K-W-L strategy (Ogle, 1986), makes use of a 3-column chart that students fill in before and after reading. Before reading, students complete the K (what I Know) section with their prior knowledge about the topic. When this is done as a collaborative activity, it also serves to expand the individual ELL's knowledge base as he/she interacts with peers who have more or different knowledge. In the second pre-reading step, students complete the W (what I Want to know) section, which helps students set a purpose for reading. The final L (what I Learned) is completed after the reading. See Figure 5.3 for an example of a K-W-L chart.

Quick Writes

In quick writing, students think of what they know about the topic to be read. They are then encouraged to write in a rambling fashion on the topic, making connections between the topic and their own experiences. The writing segment lasts for a short, designated time. Following the writing, students are invited to share their Quick Writes with each other. Here is an example of a quick write completed by a sixth grade ELL on the topic of the George Washington Bridge.

> *The George Washington Bridge is a suspension bridge. It spans the Hudson River and connects New York and New Jersey. I can see the bridge from my house and I like to watch the cars go over it. The George Washington Bridge was built by the Port Authority and has an upper level and a lower level. I read a book about a lighthouse that is under the bridge. It was there before the bridge was built.*

Table 5.4 Signal words and graphic organizers for informational text

Text structure	Key words	Graphic organizer
Description	for example	Cluster, web, map
Sequence (time)	after before next then at last finally long ago today, tomorrow, yesterday	Time line dates events
Sequence (process)	first, second, etc. next finally last	Sequence chart
Compare/ contrast	although but however in contrast compared with on the one hand, on the other hand	T–chart Common
Problem/ solution	(statement of problem followed by solution)	solution solution ← → solution solution
Cause/effect	therefore because thus since for this reason as a result consequently	effect cause ← → effect effect

Figure 5.3 K – W – L Chart

K *What do I already know?*	W *What do I want to find out?*	L *What did I learn?*

Supporting ELLs' Vocabulary Instruction

Lack of English vocabulary knowledge is one the major obstacles faced by ELLs' in their efforts to become expert readers and writers. In addition to meeting many content-specific words at the upper elementary grades level, ELLs also have to contend with the expanded use of figurative language in their reading texts. As teachers of these students, we need to provide the type of instruction that will help them overcome this obstacle. For example, it is essential that, before asking students to read a selection, we spend sufficient time developing key concepts and essential vocabulary. Likewise, after reading, it is important to clarify word meanings and deepen conceptual understanding. In this section, we will present some guiding principles governing effective vocabulary instruction and offer some suggested instructional strategies.

Guiding Principles of Vocabulary Instruction

(1) **Effective instruction integrates the known with the new.** Instructional strategies should help students connect new vocabulary to their background knowledge. Since learning words in isolation is usually ineffectual, we need to present vocabulary items in a manner that will enable students to see relation-

ships between terms. The use of graphics such as conceptual clusters is a recommended technique for helping students make relational connections. Figure 5.4 illustrates an example of a conceptual cluster.

(2) **Effective instruction makes use of meaningful repetition.** Repetition helps students remember new vocabulary. Instructional strategies should provide enough opportunities for practice in meaningful contexts. For this reason, merely giving students word lists to be memorized is usually ineffectual. It is better to use some of the suggested instructional strategies coupled with opportunities to use the target word in reading and writing throughout the day, as this allows the students to internalize the word and its meaning.

(3) **Effective instruction increases the depth of students' vocabulary knowledge.** A goal of vocabulary instruction should be to develop higher-level word knowledge. Avoid rote memorization of definitions. It is better to focus on helping students see the connections between words and concepts. An example of this would be having students use vocabulary in projects related to content area subjects such as math, science, or social studies.

Figure 5.4 Conceptual cluster

(4) **Effective instruction fosters independence**. Teach students strategies so that they can learn new vocabulary independently.

Vocabulary Instructional Strategies

(1) **Word walls.** These are displays on which the students and the teacher record significant words from stories, informational readings, or content-area textbooks. The words on the wall are available for students to refer to as they engage in various literacy and content activities throughout the day. Some teachers prepare a separate word wall for each content-area subject. ELLs can benefit from creating their own individual word walls using an opened manila folder. These individual word walls can list key vocabulary that needs to be accessible to the ELL but which the class as a whole may not need to have displayed.

(2) **Exclusion brainstorming** (Tompkins, 1998). Here the teacher, as a pre-reading activity, provides students with a list of words and a topic (from social studies or another curricular area). Working collaboratively, students decide which words on the list refer to the topic, and which do not. As they discuss and work with the words, students learn key vocabulary, acquire knowledge of the topic, and set a purpose for reading. After reading, students look at the words again and determine if their original decisions about the words were correct.

(3) **Contextual redefinition** (Cooper with Kiger, 2003). This is a prereading activity that helps provide students with the contextual information needed for learning new vocabulary. The teacher selects the key vocabulary to be learned and prepares sentences that provide appropriate clues to the meaning of each word. Initially, the words are presented to the students in isolation, and the students are asked to provide definitions. The teacher then presents the words in context, using the previously-prepared sentences. Students are then asked to make 'informed guesses' as to the meanings of the words and to provide a rationale for their definitions based on the contexts. Part of the discussion focuses on the differences between defining a word in context and defining it in isolation. In this way, less able readers can experience the thinking processes involved in defining a word from context. Finally, students check their definitions with the dictionary.

(4) **Semantic feature analysis**. Although sometimes used before reading, this activity is most effective when used after reading. Students learn vocabulary by comparing topic-related words to each other. Words from a pre-selected category (e.g. geometric figures) are listed along the left side of a grid. Features common to some of the topic words are listed along the top of the grid. Students fill in the grid, marking pluses if the topic word has the respective characteristic, minuses if the topic word does not have the characteristic, and question marks if the answer is not known. Table 5.5 is an example of a semantic feature analysis created by a group of sixth grade ELLs.

Table 5.5 Semantic feature analysis

Types of triangles						
	Line segment	All sides congruent	All angles congruent	Right angle	Obtuse angle	Acute angle
scalene	+	-	-	(+)	(+)	+
isosceles	+	-	-	-	-	+
equilateral	+	+	+	-	-	+
acute	+	-	+	-	-	+
right	+	-	-	+	-	+
equiangular	+	+	+	-	-	+

+ = shape has attribute
-   = shape does not have attribute
(+) = shape may sometimes have attribute

There are many other instructional strategies and activities that can be used to develop vocabulary knowledge for ELLs. In determining how to teach vocabulary, it is wise to be guided by the principles presented previously. Also, when providing direct vocabulary instruction, our experience leads us to exercise caution not to overload the students with large numbers of words. In the long-term, teaching a few key words essential to understanding the text will be much more effective than having students memorize long lists of definitions.

QUESTIONING THAT SUPPORTS COMPREHENSION

The pivotal place that questioning has in helping readers construct meaning from text was referred to earlier in this chapter. In this section, we present two formats for using questioning with ELLs as a means of enhancing their comprehension: *reciprocal questioning* and *question-answer-relationship* (Q-A-R).

Reciprocal Questioning

In reciprocal questioning (Tompkins, 1998), students have the opportunity to become more actively involved in the meaning-making process as they read. This occurs as students formulate questions to ask the teacher and each other based on the reading.

To use reciprocal questioning as an instructional strategy, teachers need to select a text (e.g. content-area textbook) and segment it. The length of the segment can vary from a sentence to a paragraph depending on the density of the material and the students' reading ability. (When using this with ELLs, particular attention has to be given to the prereading components such as prior knowledge and key vocabulary.) Students are then instructed to read the segment silently. After reading, the students ask the teacher questions about the text, which the teacher answers without referring back to the text. After the teacher has answered several of the students' questions, roles are switched and the teacher now asks questions of the students, who answer without referring back to the text. This is a good opportunity for the teacher to model questioning. Questions can be of all types: literal, inferential, evaluative, open-ended, those based on students' experiences, and those that relate to vocabulary. In another variation of this strategy, students and teacher can alternate asking and answering questions. When the questioning of a particular segment is complete, the teacher asks the students to make predictions as to what the content of the next segment will be. The subsequent segments of text are read silently following the same format.

Question-Answer-Relationship (QAR)

As noted in the previous section, there are different types of questions that readers may be called upon to answer. Often ELLs have difficulty in knowing where to find the source of information needed to answer a specific question. Teaching students to look for question-answer relationships (QAR) (Pearson & Johnson, 1978) can help address this problem. In QAR, students are introduced to four levels of questions (International Reading Association, 1988):

(1) **Right there.** These questions can be answered by recalling and locating information explicitly stated in the text.
(2) **Putting it together.** To answer these questions, the reader is required to find information in two or more locations in the text, making text-connecting inferences.
(3) **Author and me**. The answers to these questions require the reader to combine information in the text with personal experience.
(4) **On my own**. The answers to these questions are found in the reader's background of experience and can be answered without even reading the text.

Instruction that includes this type of analysis of the relationship between questions and answers develops ELLs' knowledge of where answers come from, and can help them improve in their ability to answer questions independently (Raphael, 1986).

PROMOTING READING FLUENCY IN ELLS

Reading fluency is the ability to read rapidly, without hesitation, and with accuracy. In silent reading, fluent readers recognize words automatically and group them in meaningful chunks increasing their ability to construct meaning from text. In oral reading, fluent readers read smoothly and with appropriate expression.

Fluency in reading is considered to be an essential step in moving from word recognition to reading comprehension. This is because fluent readers do not have to use their cognitive resources to decode words but rather can concentrate on making meaning from the text. Also, fluent readers, because they are focusing primarily on meaning, are better able to monitor and self-correct comprehension breakdowns as they occur.

For ELLs, fluent oral reading can be especially challenging because they are reading in their non-native language. Often, ELLS' lack of oral reading fluency is interpreted as poor reading ability in general. Among ELLs, it is important to recognize the difference between the oral reading of able readers with limited oral English proficiency and those whose non-fluent oral reading is indicative of lack of automatic word recognition ability and meaning making difficulties. For those students in the latter group, the struggling ELLs in upper elementary grades, their fluency problems are often exacerbated by their under-developed competence in English, which is characterized by lack of English vocabulary and by inadequate syntactical knowledge.

Helping students become fluent readers is important because of the positive relationship between reading fluency and comprehension. Some instructional strategies have been identified as being effective in building up reading fluency.

(1) **Level of text.** Choose materials for oral reading that are not too difficult for the student to read.
(2) **Read-aloud and shared reading.** Using the read-aloud and shared reading formats, provide students with a model of fluent oral reading. This can also be accomplished by having the student follow along in the reading while listening to an audiotaped version of the text. It is recommended that there is no music or sound effects on the tape. In the initial reading, the student can follow while pointing to each word as it is read. In the subsequent reading, the student can try to read along with the tape. This procedure should be repeated until the student can read the text independently.
(3) **Echo reading.** This strategy is recommended for use when working one-on-one with an ELL. Read a sentence or short section of the text pointing to the words as you read. The student follows along, and echoes the text back to you.
(4) **Silent reading before oral reading.** Give the student the opportunity to read the text silently before reading it orally.
(5) **Repeated reading.** Select a text that is between 50–200 words long, and in which the student is able to recognize most of the words. Ask the student to read the passage orally three to four times, each time focusing on improving fluency (Lerner, 2003).
(6) **Choral reading.** The students read along with you as a group (see earlier section on Shared Reading). For choral reading, choose a poem or other text that is not too long. Selections that have repetitive parts (e.g. books with repetitive passages) are especially suited to choral reading.
(7) **Readers' theater.** Students rehearse and perform a story that has been recast as

a play for an audience. Readers' theater is especially effective for developing fluency because students are motivated to reread the text repeatedly as they prepare for the performance before the audience.

USING NATIVE LANGUAGE KNOWLEDGE IN ENGLISH READING

Throughout this chapter, we have pointed out the particular needs that ELLs have as they engage in English reading. However, we also should point out that ELLs bring a unique resource to the English reading process. That resource is their bilingualism, their ability to use two languages.

Research (Jimenez, 1997) has shown us that bilinguals can use their dual language abilities to facilitate reading comprehension in either language. An example of this is the Spanish/English-speaking student who makes use of cognates. (A cognate is a word that is related in form or meaning to a word in another language.) The student came across the phrase 'lunar exploration' in reading a science text. Not being familiar with the word, 'lunar', the student was prompted by the teacher to think of a possible Spanish word that resembled 'lunar' in form. After pausing for a minute to think, the student was able to make the connection between 'luna' the Spanish word for moon and the English adjective, 'lunar.'

CONCLUSION

ELLs entering the upper elementary grades are faced with challenging literacy tasks as they encounter increasingly complex content-area texts. There is therefore a need to provide literacy instruction that will support students in their efforts to use reading in order to learn. In this chapter, we described five instructional frameworks, paralleling those previously described for writing, which can scaffold ELLs' reading development. These frameworks are: reading aloud, shared reading, guided reading, paired reading, and independent reading.

Good readers are strategic readers. In this chapter we have presented seven reading strategies that successful readers use to construct meaning: visualizing, monitoring, inferencing and predicting, identifying important information, generating and answering questions, and summarizing.

The goal of reading instruction is to help students become independent, proficient readers. Teachers can mediate ELLs' reading development and help them move toward this independence through the use of appropriate instructional strategies. In this chapter we have suggested teaching strategies with recommended guidelines for implementation that addressed specific skills such as activating prior knowledge, developing vocabulary, questioning, and promoting reading fluency.

Although we focused on students' literacy instructional needs, we also noted the unique asset that ELLs bring to the reading process. This asset, the ability to use two languages, is a resource that can serve to facilitate ELLs' reading comprehension.

English Literacy Across The Curriculum

Introduction

Integration of Language and Content

Social Studies: Learning Challenges
and Instructional Modifications

Science: Learning Challenges and
Instructional Modifications

Mathematics: Learning Challenges and
Instructional Modifications

Conclusion

CHAPTER 6
English Literacy Across the Curriculum

INTRODUCTION

Content literacy is the ability to use reading and writing for the acquisition of concepts and processes in a subject area. It includes cultural, civic, computer, media, scientific, and technological literacies. These multiple literacies require skills that extend far beyond the conventional reading and writing competencies associated with print literacy. Literacy development is part of a sociocultural process that is used to expand meaning among individuals, using cognitive and mental functioning that is embedded in an array of cultural, historical and institutional contexts (Vygotsky, 1962). In schools, content and English literacy skills and processes are interwoven into language lessons where students' oral language, reading and writing development and achievement serve to guide instruction.

What happens to students who come to school without the necessary English language proficiency to tackle the content of the subject areas in English, and who at the same time do not have the cognitive processes and strategies to keep up with their peers in the various subject areas? How are such students expected to meet the high academic standards set by state and national reform movements? How can those upper elementary ELLs achieve at grade level? Struggling ELL readers and writers need educators, especially teachers, to use approaches that prepare them to comprehend the content of their subject matter classes at the same time as they mediate their English reading and writing processes and provide meaningful contextualized language-learning situations. Through instructional adaptations, teachers make adjustments in the language demands placed on students who are struggling with literacy processes and who, through supportive teaching techniques, achieve grade level content standards and concepts. Using content area materials help ELLs to learn English because it increases student motivation, provide more opportunities for students to acknowledge and explore their own prior knowledge.

Most students would benefit from a curriculum that reflects the power and richness of scientific, social science and mathematical content. Integrating the teaching of content with language learning through collaborative learning and instructional interactions can result in students' acquisition of a variety of cognitive, linguistic and meta-cognitive processes. By applying specific teaching strategies that incorporate language functions and structures, teachers of mainstreamed ELL students can help their students progress in understanding content concepts while developing English listening, speaking, reading, and writing skills. How should teachers run a class for students who are at an intermediate level of English language proficiency and lack the cognitive skills and strategies to tackle complex content? Teachers need to employ a range of instructional activities that include vocabulary development, simplification of syntactical and discourse structures, expansion of semantic structures, use of prior knowledge, and the use of manipulatives so that content concepts and process are understood.

This chapter focuses on the identification of learning and instructional strategies for teaching content area subjects to struggling ELLs in order to increase their content knowledge (concepts), vocabulary and cognitive processes. One section provides a rationale for integrating language and content, and gives suggestions on teaching ELLs in the content areas of social studies, science and mathematics. The chapter provides a list of suggestions and examples to teachers on how to make adaptations or modifications for those ELL students who may not read, or write at an appropriate grade level, and whose difficulties may negatively affect the acquisition of concepts and processes in the content areas.

INTEGRATION OF LANGUAGE AND CONTENT

ELL students in upper elementary school are faced with a complex school curriculum encompassing several areas, such as language arts, mathematics, science, and social studies. Each content area involves specific cognitive and learning processes. Table 6:1 describes these processes. This school curriculum is composed of multiple content, processes and skills, and in many ways, the subject content and the language content (listening, speaking, reading, and writing) share distinctive linguistic and cognitive process and skills. Because of this relationship, classroom teachers can take advantage of content materials in two ways: (1) to use content materials when the main purpose is to focus on reading and writing instruction, and (2) to provide students with opportunities to read and write when the main purpose is to focus on learning specific content. Research on using reading and writing to learn, reveals the power of using print in both reading and writing to enhance learning in the content areas (Alvermann & Ridgeway, 1990; Alvermann & Swarford,1989; Fitzgerald, 1993; Vacca & Vacca, 1986).

Among the most noted benefits of using reading and writing to learn are:

(1)   improved understanding of the specific content being read or written about;
(2)   improved ability to organize, to interpret, to generalize, to perceive logical rela-
        tions;
(3)   the ability to evaluate arguments; and
(4)   the improvement of reading and writing abilities.

Table 6.1 Subject-area thinking processes

Reading	*Social science*	*Science*	*Mathematics*
Generates and organizes major ideas or concepts	Analyzes information	Observes and gathers data	Uses various mathematical functions
Supports major ideas or concepts with details	Develops concepts and generalizations	Generates hypotheses or predictions	Estimates to solve problems
Establishes interpretations supported by textual information and background knowledge	Generates hypotheses	Tests hypotheses	Uses mathematical knowledge to explain events
Makes associations between and among texts	Formulates decisions	Modifies hypotheses	Interprets events using mathematical knowledge
Makes meaningful predictions based on what has been previously read	Formulates values	Compares and contrasts	Summarizes mathematical information
Generates inferences or goes beyond the information given	Compares and contrasts	Orders and classifies	Predicts events
Reflects on, and responds and reacts to, what is being read	Offers alternatives	Measures	Integrates and connects mathematical functions and information to solve problems and to investigate the world
Uses reading various purposes or functions	Observes	Describes	Organizes mathematical information to solve problems
Reflects on and responds to the meanings being generated	Describes	Infers or draws conclusions	Draws conclusions
Evaluates the quality or value of the text	Differentiates	Develops concepts and generalizations	Categorizes information
Varies the manner in which texts are read based on different purposes, intentions, and audiences	Explains		Seeks and forms patterns
Reads, rereads or rethinks when meaning is lost or when purposes/ intentions or the needs of the audience are not met	Develops concepts and generalizations		

Adapted from S.B. Kucer *et al.* (1995)

Content Learning

Content learning is facilitated by teaching it around the following areas: (1) the students' language functions, (2) the cultural relevance of the classroom, and (3) the provision of a variety of linguistic and cognitive strategies in instruction. Language and literacy functions (e.g. organization of ideas, making predictions, use of linguistic cues) are specific uses of language for accomplishing certain purposes (Fathman *et al.*, 1992). An analysis of the kinds of function needed in subject content activities is an essential first step in choosing a language focus for the lesson. The language focus can be determined by the linguistic structures required to express each language function. By focusing on the functions used in these lessons, teachers provide students with information that has immediate practical value for understanding and communicating both in and out of the classroom. Literacy functions in the content areas require a range of strategic elements such as learning strategies, instructional strategies, learning environment, literacy/content instructional materials and technological resources. Figure 6.1 lists examples of indicators for each of these elements. Content area knowledge/information needs to be presented as relevant and interesting to students, especially to students with low literacy abilities.

Students bring varied and often rich experiences from their own cultures, and they should be encouraged to share their personal experiences when exploring

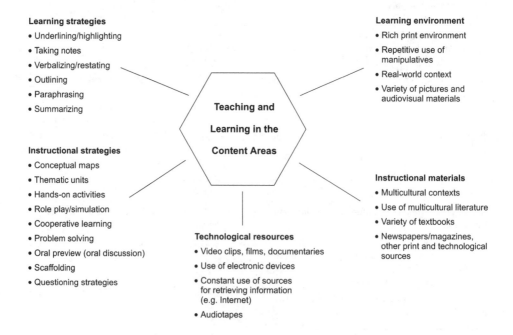

Learning strategies
- Underlining/highlighting
- Taking notes
- Verbalizing/restating
- Outlining
- Paraphrasing
- Summarizing

Instructional strategies
- Conceptual maps
- Thematic units
- Hands-on activities
- Role play/simulation
- Cooperative learning
- Problem solving
- Oral preview (oral discussion)
- Scaffolding
- Questioning strategies

Teaching and Learning in the Content Areas

Technological resources
- Video clips, films, documentaries
- Use of electronic devices
- Constant use of sources for retrieving information (e.g. Internet)
- Audiotapes

Learning environment
- Rich print environment
- Repetitive use of manipulatives
- Real-world context
- Variety of pictures and audiovisual materials

Instructional materials
- Multicultural contexts
- Use of multicultural literature
- Variety of textbooks
- Newspapers/magazines, other print and technological sources

Figure 6.1 Indicators of strategic elements in integrating literacy and content in the classroom

content topics. Personal experiences increase students' interest in a topic, make a new topic relevant to previous experience, and motivate students to explore and learn about a topic. An easy way to make teaching relevant to students is to point out the role it plays in their everyday lives. For example, a relevant topic for an integrated social studies/science lesson is to locate the native countries of ELL students on a map, identify the eating habits and food similarities and differences between these countries and those of the United States, and help students explain how eating habits affect the way people cook and live.

Whenever possible, teachers should introduce topics by using demonstrations, oral previews, real objects, pictures, films, and other visual or physical clues to clarify meaning. For example, in the science class, teachers should make use of real objects such as thermometers, telescopes, computers, and weighing scales. In the social studies class, students use maps, globes, and videos. In mathematics, students use rulers, and calculators. Teachers should plan for students to manipulate new material through hands-on activities, such as role play and simulations. An oral preview (oral discussion) on a topic using objects and visuals can facilitate reading comprehension on that topic. Oral discussions may include teacher-directed summaries, audiotapes of summaries of readings, language master cards of key words, or oral activities such as role playing. In integrating language and content, we recommend these four strategies:

(1) scaffolding instruction through appropriate comprehension monitoring, self-questioning, and small-group discussion strategies;
(2) direct instruction, especially for vocabulary development and for information-processing strategies;
(3) frequent use of thematic units, and
(4) frequent use of different types of questioning strategies to guide students to search for information.

SOCIAL STUDIES: LEARNING CHALLENGES AND INSTRUCTIONAL MODIFICATIONS

The social studies curriculum helps all children and young people to have an understanding of themselves and others in the classroom, at school, in the community, and in the world. It provides opportunities to learn about historical, social and political events, about the diversity of communities, and how people in different communities meet their needs and govern themselves.

Learning Challenges

Social studies is one of the most challenging subject areas of the school curriculum, and is closely bound to literature and to English literacy. Social studies material is often too difficult for struggling ELL students because texts are written at a readability level that is too difficult for them. Social studies instructional texts carry some level of difficulty because of the complexity of its writing style and text organization. Another difficulty relates to the vocabulary of social studies. ELL students may be unfamiliar with the social studies vocabulary and may have trouble keeping pace with native-English-speaking students, who have a broader vocabulary foundation. In addition, in most social studies classrooms there is a significant amount of reading to do, and most of the readings are expository, rather than narrative in style. Long reading passages are filled with abstract concepts and unfamiliar events and names. Moreover, some social studies books are not well-written, and often lack coherence and cohesion between sections.

At the same time, social studies classes are good tools for developing critical thinking and cognitive processes such as understanding cause–effect relationships, comparing and contrasting; collecting, organizing, interpreting data, hypothesizing; and making inferences. The cumulative nature of social studies often creates situations in which ELL students may fail to grasp concepts or ideas because they have inadequate background knowledge, gaps in instruction and more importantly, because they may lack the English literacy needed to participate using grade-level instruction and social studies classes. In addition, the cognitive academic language proficiency (CALP) of ELL students may not be sufficiently developed to cope with the demands of the social studies curriculum.

Instructional Modifications

Cognitively demanding social studies content will make sense to students only when they, according to their cognitive and literacy level, appropriately understand it. It is not recommended that social studies content should be simplified. On the contrary, what is recommended is that the content taught should be challenging and interesting and that it is delivered in a way that promotes cognitive development, especially the development of thinking skills. For struggling ELL students, teachers need to prepare a series of activities to be used *before*, *during* and *after* the lesson to make sure that students understand the content and language of the lesson.

Content materials are useful for developing reading and writing skills. This can be accomplished by presenting trade books and textbooks, as well as specific pieces of written materials from children's magazines or other children's content sources. We have found that, the greater the use of historical novels, biographies, and literature, the greater the opportunities for students to learn the content material. The power of the information included in diverse genres encourages students to acquire a broader sense of the world and its people. Literature, a major vehicle of culture, is one of the most effective language-teaching materials for students. Integrating literature that reflects students' various cultures into the different curricula serves to enhance the development of listening, speaking, reading, and writing skills. Three main steps must be taken before introducing a social studies lesson to low-literacy students. These are: (1) introduce key vocabulary, (2) provide prior knowledge, and (3) provide information about the content. A brief explanation of these three strategies follows.

Before the Lesson

Teaching Key Vocabulary in Advance

ELL students may not have sufficient English proficiency to master key words in the written text that are supposed to be part of their grade-level vocabulary, and students' understanding of the content may be affected by unfamiliarity with these key vocabulary words. If students are familiar with the core vocabulary of a particular lesson, they are more likely to understand the concepts presented through the lesson. Key vocabulary words may be written on a sheet of paper, for example, indicating the chapter in the textbook from which they came. These words are then discussed with the students as illustrated in Chapter 5, making sure that ELL students can recognize their meaning as they are used in the text and can explain their meaning in their own words.

Teachers also need to be aware that pointing out a list of vocabulary words in the textbook does not guarantee that students understand the meaning of those words as they are used in the text. Pictures or other manipulative materials may be used to get the meaning of these words across to ELL students so that they will have a comprehensive list of words that they can use in understanding the ideas or concepts presented in the lesson. Teachers need to teach students to begin thinking of ways to figure out the meaning of these words, such as locating unknown words and finding a strategy to find the meaning of the word. In addition, students should be conscious of what they can do when they encounter an unknown word so that in future situations they will be able to think through the problem themselves and resolve it independently. This could be accomplished through brainstorming activities, the use of semantic or word-webbing and teacher-led discussion. But teaching students key vocabulary words is only one aspect of the preparation involved for the social studies lesson. In order to prepare ELL students for success in the lesson, teachers must be cognizant of the background, experience, and cultural orientation of each of the students in their classrooms.

Facilitating the Use of Prior Knowledge

The language used in the expository texts of social studies books too often presumes that students have background knowledge. Providing for the development of prior knowledge is crucial for all students, particularly ELL students. These students may have had limited experience of American culture, as well as periods of interrupted schooling, which would deprive them of the considerable background knowledge that social studies textbooks assume students have. Learning is continuous and progressive, and what is learned is based on what is already known. The huge scope of information and knowledge that falls into the category of social studies, combined with the difficulty in understanding textbooks, makes background knowledge an integral element in student comprehension and learning. In order to understand new information a learner needs to be able to connect the information with what he/she already knows. How can background knowledge be considered and integrated in classroom instruction? Teachers should start with the most basic concepts and gradually develop related ideas into broader units of study.

Teachers need to draw on the students' personal experience to enable them to see how the topical area is most closely related to them.

Providing Information About the Content

The motivation for language learning arises naturally as students become involved in understanding concepts of history, geography, and anthropology and the promotion of critical concepts of American history. An introduction to a lesson helps clarify the context in which new concepts are to be presented. The teacher needs to familiarize students with the general area under consideration and to give students an idea or plan with which to make sense of the new information. For example, if the unit under consideration is 'Geography of Ancient Egypt,' the introduction to the unit can be presented in a semantic mapping format to include the areas shown below:

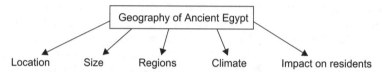

Semantic mapping uses discussion and brainstorming to construct a visual map that organizes the content. The lesson may start with a brainstorming session built around 'Ancient Egypt', a topic that is central to the lesson. Each student provides a piece of information. Although individually the students' knowledge is sparse; together it may be extensive. Thus, while not every student has the appropriate background for the lesson, the collective knowledge of the group organized through the use of semantic mapping and group discussion can develop the appropriate prior knowledge base for each student.

During the Lesson

Classroom teachers who strive to provide content information, and at the same time strengthen ELL students' academic language competence, develop and implement social studies lessons that are sensitive to the cultural and educational backgrounds of the students. Struggling ELLs benefit from instruction that:

- provides opportunities to get information about social studies in oral, written, physical or pictorial form;
- makes connections between the content being taught and the students' real-life experiences;
- uses students to provide of information about their native countries;
- activates students' background knowledge;
- provides hands-on activities;
- promotes critical thinking;
- makes language accommodations to help students learn from the information presented;

- helps students to represent information visually (e.g. graphic organizers) and to identify relationships,
- incorporates collaborative learning activities;
- provides models to help students make the transition to academic tasks, and adjusts instruction for the learning styles of different students.

Instructional strategies should involve interactive group discussion, which connects the students' knowledge to the main ideas or central concepts. Students must be actively involved in making that connection, or no learning will occur. For ELL struggling learners, we recommend: (1) collaborative groups, (2) guided reading, and (3) provision of manipulatives and audiovisual aids. In collaborative activities, ELL students are mixed with English-proficient students so that students who are having difficulty reading the textbook work alongside those who are reading at or above grade level. The roles that are assigned within groups vary depending on the purpose and focus of the task. In guided reading, the teacher needs to guide the students to understand the main ideas of the text through strategies such as:

- using necessary briefing and vocabulary development;
- identifying/writing sentences that summarize the main points of the lesson;
- skimming each section/paragraph to identify the main ideas;
- restating the idea in students' own words; and
- using restatements for summarizing the information.

By including manipulatives and audiovisual materials in the class, teachers may reach students who are at a low level of English proficiency, as well as those who are English proficient. Pictures help students to relate new vocabulary and concepts. Representing information visually benefits language learners because it highlights important topics or points out and reduces dependence on written text. Many of the concepts presented in social studies lessons are abstract ideas that may be particularly difficult for low-literacy-level English students. Pictures and videos are very important in the social studies classroom; they provide students with visual experiences that transcend language barriers. For example, describing a scene from a forest is not the same as showing a photograph or picture of the forest. The visual image makes an immediate impression on the viewer and does not rely solely on an oral or written explanation that ELL students. may not understand. Manipulatives for the social studies class includes maps, photographs, calendars, globes, videocassettes, transparencies, encyclopedias, filmstrips and weather charts.

After the Lesson

There is a 'de-briefing' stage in which the class as a whole reflects on the topic. Questions to guide the conversation may include:

- What did we learn from this lesson? Why was it useful? How can we use this knowledge in our understanding of people, events or places?

- What do information, events or ideas presented tell us about ourselves, about our values, and about our ideas?

If the assessment of the lesson reveals that students did not get the main knowledge, skills and processes of the lesson, teachers may want to repeat the topic using other readings and resources and more guided instruction. The following strategies are highly recommended:

- checking the level of the reading material; if it is too high for the student, modify or adjust it to match the ability of the student;
- reducing distracting elements in order to increase students' ability to concentrate on what they are reading;
- teaching students to use context clues to identify meanings of words and phrases they do not know;
- outlining reading materials for students using words and phrases at their ability level;
- guiding students to verbally paraphrase materials just read in order to assess their comprehension;
- guiding students to identify main points in the material in order to enhance their comprehension,
- getting students to outline, underline or highlight important points in the reading material;
- allowing students to take notes in order to increase their comprehension;
- introducing new words and their meanings to students before introducing new materials;
- giving students time to read a selection more than once, emphasizing reading comprehension.

SCIENCE: LEARNING CHALLENGES AND INSTRUCTIONAL MODIFICATIONS

Science is fundamentally an attempt to describe and explain the world. It is a way of understanding the world through observable patterns and applying these patterns through observation, the testing of hypotheses, and the designing and carrying out of an experiment, including the measurement and evaluation of data. Science education covers the following areas: earth science, life science, physical science, natural science, chemistry, and physics.

Learning Challenges

Scientific literacy is defined as an active understanding of scientific methods and of the social and economic roles of science and is built on an ability to acquire, update, and use relevant information about science. Science learning involves the use of literacy processes that are the root system for growth in scientific knowledge.

They are the means by which science content is not only learned, but conveyed, since content information is rooted in written and oral language. Scientists and science learners must be literate in the basic literacy process in order to be able to communicate effectively their ideas or discoveries. English literacy, which is a prerequisite to learn effectively about science processes, concepts, and skills, presents a problem to struggling ELLs when they try to make sense of the world in which they live in terms of their current knowledge and use of language. This process can present a problem for ELL students, who in many instances do not have the necessary English language proficiency, cognitive processes and learning strategies to be able to understand science content and processes. Science instruction should facilitate the development or understanding of science as a way of knowing and as a cognitive process. Figure 6.2 illustrates three recommended processes for exploring science content.

The science classroom provides an excellent atmosphere for developing the kinds of social and scientific behaviors that ELL students need in order to find solutions to local and global problems. However, in teaching science to ELL students, the main objectives are to make the science material understandable and meaningful, to motivate and involve the students, and to enhance the acquisition of the concepts and skills of science as well as the development of the English language. Science offers a unique way of looking at the world; it provides opportunities for asking questions, for gathering and interpreting data, and for explaining findings. Scientific thinking involves particular attitudes that include making judgments based on adequate data, striving to be rational and analytical, and maintaining a sense of wonder at the complexity and beauty of the universe.

Science is, in itself, a language, and each different branch of science (biology,

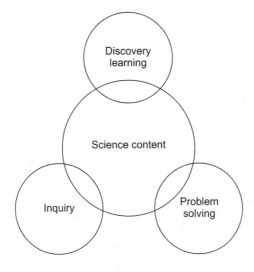

Figure 6.2 Three processes for exploring science content

physics, and chemistry) is a separate language. Science involves the acquisition of concepts and processes, specific vocabulary, phrases, and terminology. The ability to manipulate this language and its processes provides the necessary instruments for the mastery of the science curriculum. Because science is a way of thinking, it involves doing, acting, investigating, gathering, organizing, and evaluating. Struggling readers and writers may not have adequate language proficiency, or the cognitive processes or learning strategies need for all these mental steps. Science processes and skills are the tools that allow learners to gather and think about data for themselves, and involve skills such as measuring, communicating, classifying, and inferring. Students must be challenged through argument and discussion to focus on thinking skills. To become actively involved in hands-on science, they must use the tools of science, or the process-inquiry skills, which include observing, classifying, measuring, using spatial relationships, communicating, predicting, inferring, defining operationally, and formulating hypotheses. Teaching for understanding science and the language of science means that learning needs to be seen as:

- **Goal oriented:** Skilled learners are actively involved in constructing meaning and becoming independent learners.
- **Developmental:** Science content learning provides opportunities to link new information to prior knowledge.
- **Strategic:** Science knowledge provides opportunities to organize knowledge in the solution of problems and in the understanding and classification of science concepts.
- **Self guided:** Learners must develop a repertoire of effective learning strategies as well as awareness of and control of their own activities.
- **Sequential:** The acquisition or development of science knowledge occurs in phases; learners must think about what they already know, anticipate what they are to learn, assimilate new knowledge, and consolidate the knowledge in meaningful concepts.

Instructional Modifications

Research in second language acquisition indicates that a critical element in effective English instruction is access to comprehensible input in English (Krashen, 1981; Thomas & Collier, 1996, 1997). One way to provide comprehensible input is by teaching meaningful content in English, using strategies and techniques that facilitate content understanding. Emphasizing the way of discovery learning, teaching for understanding, and concept development and vocabulary development are ways to provide comprehensible input. By making use of such instructional procedures to integrate content and language instruction in the science classroom, it is expected that ELL students will increase both their understanding of key science concepts and also their English proficiency levels. Science needs to be taught in a way that is understandable, is active, and includes a meaning-making process that has relevance for multicultural students while at the same time promoting increased English language proficiency. To be successful in teaching science concepts and skills to struggling ELL students, teachers need to give simultaneous attention to the language used and the content presented. Through the use of specific teaching strategies that reflect learning and teaching principles appropriate to limited English speakers, teachers can help students, who are acquiring English to understand basic science content while improving their English skills. Thinking skills can be developed through teacher–student questioning, or through scheduled activities such as problem solving and decision making. The science classroom must provide inquiry activities, and the development of concepts and vocabulary. These three areas are briefly discussed in the next paragraphs.

Provision of Inquiry Activities

Students build scientific knowledge through their own efforts by thinking about and applying science concepts, and formulating complete thoughts in English. In a discovery environment, students have the opportunity to find the answers to the questions they themselves pose about a topic. Students investigate a topic of their own choosing, rather than one recommended by the teacher. They identify the problem, hypothesize causes, design the procedures or experiments, and conduct research to try to solve the problem. At the beginning, ELL students need guidance to formulate complete thoughts and to express their questions and answers. Students need to see science as an exploration of unknown concepts and processes. Problem-solving situations show this face of the science classroom. In problem solving, students must select and order varied types of data, using concepts that they already know to guide their search for answers to questions. This process leads to an understanding of new concepts and their relationships. Associated with this process are the efforts ELL students make to convert these experiences to appropriate language.

Problem-solving situations encourage discussion, which is necessary for ELL student's language development. Unfortunately, most talk in a science class comes from teachers, not from the students. In typical courses, students serve as scribes, taking notes, and asking questions for clarification. None of these activities engages students' minds as effectively as does vigorous argument and discussion.

Teachers should provide a variety of resources to support students' discovery activities: materials for science laboratory investigations, reference books, newspapers, magazines, access to libraries for additional materials, classroom visits from specialists in the community, field trips, films, and computer programs. The science curriculum needs to stress the cognitive processes of observing, inferring, predicting, hypothesizing and experimenting. These skills provide a rich environment for simultaneous cognitive and linguistic development. The use of a pre-writing activity such as semantic webbing is also an excellent task for students before they read, discuss, or conduct an experiment. Students may list items first and web later; or they may web as they list, creating new strands as categories occur to them.

Development of Concepts

ELL students with a low literacy level may have a repertoire of basic scientific concepts in need of further development. They need to expand these and add other concepts and processes related to the science grade-level curriculum. When students are provided with appropriate conceptual development strategies, such as problem solving, they can expand their concepts, ideas, and knowledge. Providing concept development strategies allows students to investigate a topic of their own choosing, with teachers acting as facilitators. Students identify a problem, hypothesize causes, design procedures or experiments, and conduct research to try to solve the problem. They work together, sharing information while practicing their language, negotiating meaning and practicing critical thinking skills.

Vocabulary Development

Science content material deals with the learning and application of new vocabulary. Specialized vocabulary is closely tied to the specific content of science. Knowing vocabulary is not just identifying the scientific jargon; it includes the ability to use the vocabulary of science to make informed decisions about science issues that would affect society as well as students personally. It is important to incorporate vocabulary development into science lessons, and to ensure that students understand the science concepts being introduced. At the same time, science provides a good opportunity to improve English literacy skills. The introduction of vocabulary words should be limited, so as not to overwhelm students with too many definitions/meanings. Vocabulary can best be introduced using real objects, pictures, and other visual devices. Ways in which teachers can facilitate students' understanding of the English terms or names to be used in a lesson include:

- helping students to label with stickers the items to be used in an experiment;
- verbally describing what the students are doing; and
- using language that is appropriate for the students' proficiency level.

Activities to help students learn vocabulary in a science reading include:

- finding and underlining the key words in the reading selection:
- writing the meaning of the words even if it is in their own language;
- writing the words in individual sentences;
- using the word in context with the person sitting next to the student.

Using Visual Devices and Manipulatives

Visual and technological devices help to clarify the context in which new concepts are to be presented. Teachers need to familiarize students with the new area or topic under consideration, and to provide them with visual and technological resources to help them acquire new information. For example, there are many videos available on the market that are useful for motivating students on the unit under discussion, or as a tool to activate prior knowledge or to provide information about the content under study.

Using Collaborative Learning Strategies

To ensure effective learning, science educators must employ strategies that make students active participants in their own learning, not passive receivers of knowledge. Collaborative strategies are effective instructional tools for improving students' participation and academic performance in all subjects, but especially in science. Collaborative strategies in the science classroom are particularly important in encouraging students to work together through inter-student communication. These strategies promote collaboration among students' peer groups or teams of students who are stronger in English language proficiency and can help those with weaker language skills to perform the necessary learning tasks. Students, who work together effectively in heterogeneous language groups, take responsibility for each other's learning and develop a positive attitude toward collaboration. It is important for each student to have a role to play in the completion of the particular problem-solving activity (recorder, illustrator, material collector, or reporter, for example).

MATHEMATICS: LEARNING CHALLENGES AND INSTRUCTIONAL MODIFICATIONS

Mathematics instruction for ELL students needs to take into consideration the students' literacy level and mathematics knowledge in order to provide experiences that bridge gaps in mathematics literacy and prepare them for success in future mathematics course work and experiences (Carrasquillo & Rodriguez, 2002). Mathematics learning is a very important component of cognition because understanding and problem solving not only help students to learn mathematical concepts, but also to improve their ability to think, reason, and solve problems. Mathematics' concepts such as money, measurement, size, shape, addition, and subtraction come into play in everyday life, and students must be comfortable with mathematical processes and functions. For struggling readers and writers, beginning in kindergarten and continuing through every grade, skills such as measuring, computing, estimating, and verifying are all taught together, often in the context of real-world situations. As indicated in Table 6.2, the field of mathematics includes many areas, skills and processes, including reasoning, number, numeration, operations, representation and patterns.

Learning Challenges

Students must be taught to understand and solve mathematical problems. To achieve in mathematics means that all students should learn to value mathematics,

Table 6.2 Mathematics in the upper elementary grades

Mathematical reasoning
     analyze mathematical situations;
     make conjectures;
     gather evidence;
     argue.

Number and numeration
     develop an understanding of the multiple uses of numbers;
     communicate mathematically;
     use numbers in the development of mathematical ideas.

Operations
     use mathematical operations and relationships;
     understand mathematical processes.

Representation
     use mathematical modeling/multiple representations;
     provide a major link between the abstraction and the real world;
     describe and compare objects and data.

Patterns and functions
     develop mathematical knowledge and processes;
     appreciate the value of mathematical generalizations;
     describe patterns efficiently.

communicate mathematically, reason mathematically, and become confident in their ability to do mathematics, as well as to become mathematical problem solvers. Struggling ELL readers and writers fall short in their mathematical abilities (problem solving, critical thinking, and reasoning). A deficiency in language and cognitive development may interfere with a student's ability to solve mathematics tasks. Students also need to learn the language of mathematics and must be able to express its concepts and skills so that they may solve ordinary life problems. Students are not only expected to perform mathematical functions, they also have to read, analyze, and interpret information in order to solve mathematical problems.

Every student creates a personal understanding of mathematics and the world through a process of experimentation, conjecture and discussion of the ideas in the context of real-world situations. ELL students are often quick to develop the social language skills that enable them to communicate with their peers outside of the classroom. However, within an academic context, this basic proficiency is inadequate because ELL students may be inexperienced with the mathematical world or the terminology and writing styles particular to mathematics. These students may not be prepared to perform the higher-order language and cognitive tasks required in rigorous academic content courses, especially in the area of mathematics.

The Language of Mathematics

The language of mathematics is abstract, difficult, and precise. The language register for mathematics is composed of meanings appropriate for the communication of mathematical ideas, together with the vocabulary terms used, the specific syntax and semantics, and the appropriate discourse needed to understand and express ideas and structures. Mathematics is a language that expresses the size, order, shape, and relationships among quantities. It has an established vocabulary, syntax, semantics, and discourse based on representational symbols in its various branches including arithmetic, algebra, geometry, calculus, and number theory. The question raised by mainstream educators is how to ensure that the language of mathematics is effectively taught and communicated to ELL students when they do not have the necessary English language proficiency, English literacy or cognitive strategies to understand mathematics content, processes and skills.

Because struggling readers and writers have unique needs, designed activities and teaching strategies should be incorporated into the school mathematics program in order for all students to have the opportunity to develop their mathematics potential regardless of any lack of proficiency in the language of instruction. The National Council of Teachers of Mathematics (NCTM) standards emphasize that mathematics should make sense to children, and that children should become thinkers through activities such as classifying, generalizing and hypothesizing (NCTM, 1989). The national mathematics academic standards challenge teachers to teach all students using active learning strategies designed to develop comprehension in solving mathematical problems.

The subject of mathematics has vocabulary words and language structures that may interfere with ELL students' understanding and processing of mathematics concepts and skills. A significant number of mathematics terms and terminology will be new to most students. Carrasquillo and Rodriguez (2002) list vocabulary difficulties, including the following:

- complexity of concepts: *tenths, mixed numbers, whole numbers, three-quarters;*
- complex set of phrases to describe a concept: *least common denominator;*
- syntactical complexity: *eight divided by four, ten is divided by two;*
- logical connectors: *four plus four is eight,* and
- semantics: *common, equal, irrational, column, table.*

Another challenge for ELLs is the verbalization of a mathematical problem. However, we have found that verbalizing a problem helps ELLs to focus on the identification of the main ideas and to organize their thinking. The process of explanation enables them to revisit their thinking and to confirm their thoughts. It also serves to clarify wrong assumptions that lead them to incorrect responses. Educators are encouraged to provide opportunities for ELL students to verbalize and discuss specific ideas that will later be included in the mathematics lesson. Teachers need to encourage students to talk to one another as they work in pairs on these activities. In order for mathematical language to develop and be mastered, it must be used. We recommend that teachers encourage the use of English, but do not discourage students from using their first language.

Instructional Recommendations

It is essential that the mathematics classroom environment is structured and organized to facilitate understanding and process development. Teachers need to prepare the classroom in such a way that the appropriate language and communication are used to communicate concepts, processes, and applications of mathematics. For struggling readers and writers, the following areas need to be emphasized in the development of the content and process of mathematics: (1) constructing meanings, (2) solving problems in meaningful situations, (3) using thinking strategies to learn basic facts, and (4) the integration of mathematics with the other content areas. The National Council of Teachers of Mathematics recommends (NCTM, 1989) instruction that fulfills the following basic student goals:

- learning to value mathematics;
- becoming confident in their ability to do mathematics;
- becoming mathematical problem solvers;
- learning to communicate mathematically;
- learning to reason mathematically.

The NCTM goals redirect the school curriculum to integrate language and mathematical skills within the same framework. Providing students with carefully planned instruction is a responsibility of effective teaching and effective schooling. The following instructional recommendations are useful in helping low-literacy ELLs to understand and succeed in the grade level mathematics curriculum.

Help Students to Construct Their Own Understanding

Students must construct for themselves personal understandings of mathematics concepts and processes. Table 6.3 provides two examples of problems that fourth graders had to solve in a state mathematics-criterion reference test.

At the exam, students were alone, making sense of mathematics questions such as the above. It is hoped that teachers prepared the students to successfully complete those questions by providing instruction that engaged them in the construction of mathematical understanding through the use of group work, open discussions, presentations, and explanations of mathematical ideas. Instead of students passively memorizing and using only rote memory, students should be actively engaged through various modes of communication, analyzing and solving mathematical problems. This approach enables students to share mathematical

Table 6.3 Fourth grade mathematics word problem

A sign at Neno's Market reads:

> **Apples**
> **$ 0.75 each**
> **$2.50 bag of 5**
>
> *Neno's Market*

Part 1

Which is the *least expensive* way to buy 5 apples at the market?
5 separate apples or 1 bag of 5 apples?

Answer: 1 bag of apples

Show your work.

1 bag = $2.50	$0.75	$3.75
	x 5	-2.50
	$3.75	$1.25

Part 2

What is the *least amount of money* someone will need to buy exactly 12 apples?

Answer: $6.50

Show your work.

$2.50 (5 apples)	$0.75 (1 apple)	$5.00
$2.50 (5 apples)	$0.75	$1.50
$5.00 (10 apples)	$1.50	$6.50

problems and to identify the use of metacognitive strategies in their solution. The focus of the process is on building an understanding so that it can be transferred to other situations. Burns (1992) recommends the following strategies:

- introduce mathematical concepts to students in real-world contexts;
- develop number sense and an understanding of the relationships between the operations;
- integrate arithmetic with the other strands of the mathematics curriculum;
- build on children's own ways of thinking and language for describing their thinking;
- rely heavily on estimating mathematical computation;
- encourage students to verbalize a thought in order to find their own ways to do mathematics calculation.

Higher-level skills are required to apply problem-solving, mental arithmetic, and estimation to situations. To develop this knowledge, students must continually be placed in situations in which they need to know and have the means to determine simple facts. The following example asks students to use high level thinking skills to verbalize the operation.

> If you don't know the sum of 42 + 18, how could you figure out the answer?

In order to solve this problem, teachers may use manipulatives such as objects to facilitate the understanding and solution of the problem. We recommend that teachers encouraging discussion in order to expose students to explaining and defending their responses. The more students can verbalize their understanding of the processes of mathematical operations, the easier it is for them to solve mathematical problems. In addition, writing helps students reflect on and clarify their thinking.

Help Students Develop Problem-solving Strategies

Students initially need to be guided to build understanding of mathematics so that they can construct their own knowledge with the focus on valuing the mathematics process. In using problem-solving strategies, students need to develop their own procedures in which they can discuss, explain, modify, and write about their understanding. In solving a mathematics problem with struggling ELLs, a step-by-step problem-solving process is recommended. The suggested plan requires four steps:

(1)   understanding the problem;
(2)   developing a plan that students feel will solve the problem;
(3)   trying the plan to see if it works;
(4)   looking at the results to see if these results make sense for that problem. If the results do not make sense, students go back and analyze the problem again.

The following strategies are recommended for students who are struggling readers and have difficulties in solving mathematical word problems:

- have students read the math word problem silently, and then ask them to identify the mathematical operation required;
- provide word problems that require a one-step process, making certain that the sentences are short;
- have students restate the mathematical word problem in their own words;
- teach students to look for key words that indicate the mathematical operation;
- have students analyze the steps that are required to solve the word problem (What is given? What is asked?);
- ask students to write a sentence after reading the word problem;
- provide students with two ways to solve a mathematics problem; such as:

(1) give students a word problem first: *seven mangos plus twelve mangos add to nineteen mangos,*

(2) gradually change the word problem to a number: 7+12=19.

Use Literature

Literature is a good vehicle for the development of mathematics content and process. Stories such as *Magic Money Machine* (Nelson, 1990), and the *Anno's Math Games* (Anno, 1999) help students explore new concepts through active participation, integrating new ideas, and predicting new outcomes. Literature can serve as that link between using concrete materials and abstract activities. Story problems are often used to motivate specific areas of mathematics content and require the development of specific problem-solving strategies. The following example presents an activity in which students need to understand the problem to perform the required task.

Task:	Draw a picture to depict the events of the story
Problem:	Joseph had some toy cars. He gave one half of the toys to his friend Pedro. Now Joseph has nine cars. How many did he have to start with?

Review Students' Literacy Skills

Teachers need to review vocabulary, reading and writing skills to facilitate the understudying of mathematics concepts and process. The most prevalent language difficulties for non-native English speaking students include the understanding of lexical items, and the use of comparative terms or structures. Before the mathematics lesson, the teacher should make sure that students have enough understanding of the key words of the lesson (e.g. terms, vocabulary) to be able to follow the mathematical concepts and processes that will be introduced in the lesson. Activities such as semantic mapping, reviewing prior knowledge and experiences, brainstorming, and defining words in context are suggested activities for ensuring that the vocabulary to be used in the math lesson is understood by everyone, including ELL students. The teacher questions and asks students to respond by rephrasing the information in their own words. Specific question may include:

- Do you understand the problem or operation asked for?
- Restate the problem in your own words.
- Explain what are you trying to find out.
- How do you think you might solve the problem?

Use Manipulatives

Manipulatives serve as concrete representations of mathematical concepts. Incorporating the use of concrete materials enables teachers to make better assessment and to meet the needs of individual students as they construct their mathematical knowledge. Manipulatives need to be seen as the bridge to make the connections between the concrete objects, pictures or technological devices, and the mathematics concepts. To serve as manipulatives, teachers can utilize everything from color tiles, beans, rods, and number blocks to fingers and toes. The materials need to be accessible to students for use in counting, classifying, patterning, constructing, and exploring. Their value lies in the ways in which they are incorporated into the class lessons. Manipulatives, when used effectively, aid in contributing to conceptualization and understanding. Progression in concept development starts from the concrete, and then moves to the abstract.

CONCLUSION

Reading and writing play an important role in classroom learning. These two literacy areas have the potential to shape ELLs thinking and learning in many powerful ways. The content areas of social studies, science and mathematics have unique language and literacy processes that are usually not mastered by struggling ELLs. These students often lack strategies – the kind of literacy strategies necessary to learn effectively. This chapter has provided educators with instructional guidance to provide explicit instruction in the development and use of literacy strategies in these three content areas.

One of the most important ways that teachers respond to the literacy needs of ELLs is to scaffold instruction so that learners become aware and competent with strategies that support learning. Recommended instructional interventions included scaffolding, support and guidance to build ELLs' confidence and competence in English reading and writing. Scaffolding literacy strategies such as explanations, modeling, and practice can help struggling readers and writers to cope with the comprehension and processing problems that they encounter in academic texts and in instruction in general.

CHAPTER 7

A Framework for Assessing English Literacy Among Struggling ELLs

A Framework for Assessing English Literacy Among Struggling English Language Learners

INTRODUCTION

Assessment has always been and probably always will be a major component of schooling. Because of its crucial role, assessment must be reliable, valid, and ongoing. Assessment provides information on the academic preparation of students, including pre-academic skills, English language proficiency, literacy development, and the acquisition of knowledge and skills in the various content areas. Administrators, teachers, staff developers, students, and parents need assessment information to determine appropriate program placement and instruction, as well as for the monitoring of students' progress. Accurate and effective assessment of struggling ELLs is essential to ensure that information provided is used in providing instructional interventions to these students. One of the areas of assessment of most relevance to ELLs is the assessment of literacy.

The assessment of literacy is a complicated process and it is even more complex when we are compiling information about struggling ELLs because this information is needed to identify students' level of English language and literacy development and achievement in order to place them in appropriate instructional settings and to provide effective instructional interventions. Usually, the struggling ELL has an intermediate level of English language proficiency, is below grade level in reading, writing, and usually in math and other content areas, and scores low on standardized tests. In addition, he/she may not have developed the full range of cognitive and learning strategies required for effective reading and writing.

As we have said several times in this book, struggling ELLs rely too much on the use of graphophonemics/letter sounds, under-utilize context, and have difficulty monitoring meaning (Kucer, 2001, Goodman, 1996). In consequence, they do not understand what they read and have difficulties in writing meaningful text. These are the students who have conversational fluency in English but lack the academic skills they need to compete with native English speakers. The questions are:

- How do we assess them?
- What type of assessment should be used for instructional and accountability purposes?

This chapter provides a theoretical framework to answer these questions. The chapter provides information on three main areas: (1) the assessment of English language learners, (2) assessment of literacy for instructional purposes and (3) the assessment of literacy for accountability purposes.

THE ASSESSMENT OF ENGLISH LANGUAGE LEARNERS

Assessment is the process of obtaining, collecting and describing information on students' linguistic, cognitive, and academic progress for the purpose of making educational decisions and of developing accountability in measuring progress indicators, aligned to national, state and local academic standards. Effective assessment ensures ELLs' access to appropriate instruction to meet their linguistic and educational needs. However, the assessment of ELLs has been difficult, in part because of the need to identify various levels of knowledge and proficiency in English in addition to assessing what students do and do not know about reading and writing. However, in the case of ELLs, the primary purpose of assessment is the documentation of students' learning to inform and improve teaching and learning in order to ensure that students are on course to becoming literate and able to participate in English language classroom settings.

For ELLs, one of the most assessed areas is literacy. Literacy relates to the ability to construct meaning in any of the forms used in the cultural setting to create and convey meaning (Alvermann & Phelps, 1998). Literacy is dynamic and multidimensional in nature. Kucer (2001: 4–5) indicates that 'becoming literate means learning to effectively, efficiently, and simultaneously control the linguistic, cognitive, sociocultural, and developmental dimensions of written language in a transactive fashion.' This multidimensional nature of literacy involves the employment of a variety of mental processes and strategies. Strategies, which are usually self-regulatory and consciously applied to construct meaning, represent those cognitive processes or behaviors that the individual engages in when creating meaning from and through written discourse (Tompkins, 2001; Harris & Hodges, 1995). These cognitive strategies driven by print, background, and purpose guide the reader's interaction with print and the construction of meaning (Kucer, 2001, Smith, 1971). The literacy meaning-making process requires students to develop the ability to establish relationships between: (1) vocabulary knowledge and comprehension, (2) prior knowledge and comprehension, (3) active engagement with text and comprehension, and (4) metacognitive awareness and comprehension.

Before we address the issue of how to assess and monitor ELLs' English literacy, we need to consider some observations about assessment related to this population,

ELLs may not have an Advanced Level of English Language Proficiency/ Development

To be proficient in a second language means to communicate effectively or understand ideas or thoughts through the different systems of the language: phonology, morphology, syntax, semantics and discourse. Knowledge of the English language is necessary to enable students to participate in all school and community activities offered in English. Mastery of language and literacy provides students with the tools to process different types of information in areas such as literature, science, social studies, and mathematics. We have observed that struggling readers and writers have not conquered all these dimensions of English literacy, and are often behind in their ability to use the various learning strategies to tackle the reading and writing meaning-making process.

Programs need to be designed to give all students, including struggling ELLs, the language and cognitive skills they need to take advantage of opportunities that are available to their English-speaking peers both at school and in the community. The language and cognitive skills necessary for students to participate in the English-speaking community should be clearly addressed in the assessment and in the curriculum. In addition, students should also develop social language skills needed to take advantage of linguistic and academic opportunities both in school and outside the school. These oral and literacy skills need to be assessed and taught throughout the school curriculum.

Assessment Informs Instruction

Assessment identifies the academic strengths and needs of students for the purpose of outlining appropriate curriculum and instruction. This assessment is used to determine students' gains in the language and literacy skills needed to succeed in a grade-level mainstream classroom, and to follow the academic and literacy progress of students in a given domain.

Assessment measures are part of instruction, and teachers often use this information to make instructional decisions based on the reflected strengths and needs of their students. As we say repeatedly throughout this chapter, assessment guides instruction and instruction provides the foundation for assessment. Using a variety of assessment tools and activities enable teachers to individualize instruction to meet the academic demands of their students.

The Assessment of Struggling ELLs Should Include a Multiple Measure Approach

Policy makers, educators and politicians rely on assessment results to identify effective schools and effective teaching. Because of its complex role, assessment requires a multiple-measure approach including formal (standardized tests) and informal (authentic tools) measures. Because of the English language demands and the many academic challenges that ELLs encounter, the use of 'high stakes assessment' alone may not provide a complete picture of what these students really know and the progress they have made. Current tools for assessment range from informal teacher-made measures (observations, checklists, rubrics) to formal measures (standardized, criterion referenced). State and school districts promote 'high stakes tests,' while teachers often use a variety of other assessment tools to monitor literacy development and to understand the day-to-day performance of their students. This combination of different measures of assessment works for the benefit of everyone, but is especially helpful in providing an adequate picture of the strengths and needs of struggling ELLs.

Assessment of ELLs Should Include Alternative Assessment Systems that Capture the Linguistic Range of Students, and Build on What They Can Do

It has been frequently reported that the current 'high stakes tests' overlook or ignore ELLs' backgrounds, levels of language proficiency and years of experience in the uses of English for learning purposes. Thus, it is recommended that schools develop their own batteries of authentic assessment to supplement the standardized assessment information. Assessment consists of finding out what students know or can do in order to show growth and inform instruction. In addition to the one/two year standardized assessment, assessment must include regular evidence of students' learning as they perform real-world tasks. This approach helps teachers to connect teaching, and learning in meaningful ways. This assessment practice reflects a view of instruction that is more sensitive to the natural growth of students acquiring English. For example, standardized multiple choice tests are notable in showing the range of students' abilities (Stiggins, 1988; O'Malley & Valdez Pierce, 1996). In many instances, ELLs do not achieve grade level scores, and if these scores are not analyzed from the perspective of strengths and weaknesses, the results can give the impression that these students are not learning. ELLs' growth needs to be analyzed in a continuum based on progress made over months or years. A continuum means that students' progress is assessed by comparing where they were when they arrived in school with their progress achieved throughout the years. Even if students are not at grade level, growth should be seen as effective learning.

Assessment Provides Students and Parents with Clear and Specific Testing Guidelines

For language-minority students and parents, information about assessment is crucial for effective collection of information about students' achievement. It is important that parents receive sufficient information about how assessment is implemented in their children's schools. This information should include:

(1)   the fact that the English language will be the language used in the testing;
(2)   the type of tests students will be required to take;
(3)   the content, areas and skills included in the test;
(4)   the format of the test (e.g. multiple choice, essay);
(5)   guidelines/tips for test-taking success.

In affluent school districts, parents demand that the type of assessment procedures and assessment results are fully explained to them. If parents are not satisfied with the assessment procedures, they may question the school district policies and request changes in the ways their children are assessed. Although many parents of ELLs are not involved in their children's' assessment, school districts need to be more aggressive in informing parents about assessment purposes, instruments, and formats.

Another important aspect of assessment is program evaluation, in which the quality of the instruction provided is analyzed and any areas of weakness are identified. This evaluation results in program improvement because it is based on criteria for the program to meet the standards set by the curriculum and by the district or the state. In addition, the information provides policy makers with information about students, programs, and the level of academic and effective teaching in the school district.

ASSESSMENT OF LITERACY FOR INSTRUCTIONAL PURPOSES

The most important role of assessment is to guide instruction. Nitko (2001) provides some recommendations on how to use assessment data for instruction. These recommendations have been slightly modified to be applicable to the teaching of ELLs. Appropriate assessment:

- Describes the language proficiency level and educational developmental level of each ELL student. This information can be used to modify or adapt instruction to accommodate the needs of the individual student.
- Describes specific qualitative strengths and weaknesses in students. These strengths vary from one curriculum area to another. This information can be used to remediate weaknesses and capitalize on strengths.
- Describes the extent to which a student has attained the prerequisites needed (e.g. academic level of English language proficiency) to go on to new or advanced learning. These results are combined with students' classroom performance to make recommendations for instructional and program placement.

- Describes commonalities among students. This information helps in grouping students for more efficient instruction.
- Students' performances in specific areas of the curriculum help to describe students' accomplishments with respect to specific instructional targets. This information is useful in making immediate instructional decisions.
- Provides students with operational descriptions of what kinds and levels of performances are expected of them. These expectations help students to gather information and describe how they can work toward their fulfillment.
- Provides students and parents with feedback about students' progress toward learning goals. This information is then used to establish a plan for home and school to work together.

A common criticism is that standardized assessment usually does not inform instruction. The concern has been that even, those 'best standardized tests' do not really provide an authentic view of students' strengths, usually what they show is the weaknesses of students based only on one discrete point in time (Darling-Hammond, 1994; O'Malley & Valdez Pierce, 1996). What has been proposed is the use of a combination of standardized and other authentic measures to provide a better picture of students' language and literacy development and level of academic achievement (Cummins, 2001). Standardized assessment plays an important role when used in conjunction with authentic assessment. Standardized data can inform teachers of broad language and literacy areas that students have mastered, or areas in need of development. The advantages of using a combination of assessment tools for instruction is that they provide teachers with the opportunity to observe a variety of oral and written products and thinking skills in the setting of the classroom environment, and the assessment of knowledge and growth of language and literacy acquisition and development over a period of time (O'Malley & Valdez Pierce, 1996). Teachers will then use their own holistic evaluations of the various authentic materials and compare them with results of the various standardized tests given to the students. In addition to the standardized assessment of academic English literacy, various daily or weekly tools must be administered and analysed on order to ensure a variety of oral, reading and writing experiences in the setting of the classroom environment, and the assessment of knowledge and growth of literacy attainment over a period of time (Cohen, 1994).

Accurate and complete assessment of ELLs requires teachers to have sufficient information to answer the following questions:

- Do students read or write in their native language?
- What is students' overall grade level of academic development?
- What specific mastery/performance of English grammar, vocabulary, listening comprehension do students have? What are the language and literacy skills they lack?
- Can students participate in highly-focused English oral language activities?
- Can students read and write English at a grade level similar to that of their mainstream/native English speakers peers?

- What is the level of English reading and writing that students are good at? What are the areas/skills they lack?

Teachers can answer these questions by using diagnostic and evaluation tools within the classroom setting as well as information provided in standardized data. This information will help teachers to provide instructional strategies to students to help them meet the specific learning targets of the curriculum. It will also help teachers in making day-to-day instructional decisions in meeting students' immediate learning targets. In which areas/skills of English reading and writing do students demonstrate proficiency? In which areas/skills are the students lacking? Teachers can organize these pieces of information/data in an 'assessment portfolio' to show the students' progress on a continuum.

In preparing administrators and teachers for using assessment to guide instruction and for gaining an overall knowledge of ELLs' strengths and weaknesses, a profile of English language development is recommended. The following section looks at the information to be collected about students.

A PROFILE OF ELLs' ENGLISH LANGUAGE PROFICIENCY AND DEVELOPMENT

Teachers cannot assume that, because ELLs are in mainstream classrooms, they are proficient in the English language and have a well-developed knowledge of the structure and form of the English language (vocabulary, syntax, morphology). Students' knowledge and experience with language must be identified so that instruction can build on existing language skills. It is important for educators to know what experience and knowledge students have with the English language, as well as with their native language. Knowing the students' level of language acquisition in their primary language and in English is helpful in identifying areas of strength. Students' knowledge and experience of English language can be assessed informally using instruments such as self-assessment questionnaires, written samples, and oral and written protocols. If necessary, teachers can ask the English as a second language (ESL) coordinator or the English language arts coordinator for standardized instruments to further verify the English language mastery of their students.

Levels of English language proficiency can be measured using a language proficiency test. Common English proficiency tests include, among others, The Basic Inventory of Natural Language or BINL (CHECpoint Systems), Language Assessment Battery – Revised or LAB-R (New York City Department of Education), Language Assessment Scales or LAS (Linguametrics Group), Maculitis Assessment Program or MAC (Jean D'Arcy Maculitis), New York State English as a Second Language Achievement Test or NYSESLAT, and The Second Language Oral Test of English or SLOTE (Alemany Press). Identifying a student's level and growth of English language involves the student's holistic ability in a language, generally showing the extent to which a student has sufficient language proficiency to learn through that second language.

It is important to assess and analyze how long students have been engaged in learning English in school. Information is also needed in terms of identifying and describing the type of instructional program students were enrolled in before coming to the mainstream classroom. This information helps teachers to understand that if students are struggling with English literacy, it is not because they are struggling readers but due to their brief experience with the English language. If a student has had four or more years of English and still has problems in learning, perhaps those academic difficulties are not related to lack of English experience, but are related to other dimensions of literacy and learning.

Schools need to assess how students use English on a daily basis, which components of language they use and for which purposes, which language students value the most, and how they use language to accomplish specific, personal and meaningful tasks. For example, what language do they use when talking to family members, or to their friends? Do they speak consistently in one language or do they switch back and forth from one language to another. Do they use English outside the classroom?

There is also a need for the identification of personal and cultural characteristics. It is the school's responsibility to take into account the cultural, political, and personal characteristics of the students as the curriculum is developed in terms of planning activities that are purposeful and meaningful to these students. Assessing or identifying students' political reasons for being in the United States and validating those experiences is a good way of making sure that educators, especially teachers, know their student population. This information will help to minimize conflicts among students from different groups and will help to ensure that all students are respected and accepted regardless of their cultural and political backgrounds. A needs assessment of students' political and cultural backgrounds is recommended, and is even more necessary if students are struggling in school.

This profile may also assess students' educational background. Students' educational background and attitudes toward education need to be considered as teachers engage in identifying work that will help students achieve goals that will give students a sense of purpose, and progress. This information provides additional information to the teacher in terms of students' motivation, level of concentration and specific themes or interest areas. For example, once teachers have identified appropriate functions of reading and writing, they should develop a checklist to identify the specific behaviors of reading and writing tasks. Each task should be evaluated using this checklist.

ASSESSING ELLs' ACADEMIC ORAL LANGUAGE DEVELOPMENT

Oral language assessment of upper elementary ELLs captures students' ability to make complex meanings explicit in the oral mode in decontextualized settings, especially in the content areas. Academic oral language consists of the ability to understand and speak English to accomplish specific tasks (describing, explaining, informing, comparing, debating, evaluating, persuading) across various content areas and domains. Comprehension means understanding everyday conversation and normal classroom discussions with fluency. Fluency refers to the ability to use speech in everyday conversation and classroom discussions in an easy and effortless way, like a native speaker. For struggling ELLs, oral social language develops rapidly, especially pronunciation and fluency. Oral academic language functions (e.g. describing, comparing, evaluating) are those that are critical for success in grade-level classrooms (Cummins, 1982; 2001) and can be used across the content areas. It is important to emphasize that many ELLs may not have the fully-developed oral language needed to complete grade-level academic tasks, especially those related to the following:

- oral language demands in the content areas such as oral presentations, panel presentations, explaining the findings of a science experiment, describing the steps of a mathematical problem;
- use of a variety of language patterns and structures such as the use of past tense verbs, word order in negative sentences, prepositions);

Table 7:1 Assessing academic oral language

Academic language function	Assessment activities
Informing	Retell a short story.
	Report information gathered by watching a film.
Comparing and contrasting	After reading information about two countries, describe similarities and differences between the two countries.
	Develop a graphic organizer to show similarities and contrasts.
Justifying and persuading	Read a newspaper editorial and present your own point of view.
	Study an algebra equation and provide evidence supporting it.
Solving a problem	Describe steps in solving a problem.
	Describe problem-solving procedures in a science experiment.
Synthesizing	Take ideas from three literature texts and summarize the information.
Evaluating	Explain the verification of a science experiment.
	Indicate reasons for agreeing with the end of a short story.

- understanding content area concepts acquired through oral resources such as a film, a video, a lecture;
- understanding key specialized vocabulary: e.g. mathematics' language, scientific terms.

Assessment of academic oral language should focus on students' ability to interpret and convey meaning for authentic purposes in individual learning/academic contexts. In assessing a student's English oral language, we can start by asking questions such as: Does the student use language to describe concepts or ideas? Does the student have sufficient vocabulary to explain a literature situation or a mathematics problem? Does the student have the language structures needed to sustain a conversation or to share or compare information? Is the student able to provide an opinion on a topic or an issue? Table 7.1 illustrates examples of academic functions and assessment activities for identifying the strengths and needs of struggling ELLs.

Because teachers are involved in many instructional and assessment activities during the academic year, and they do not have extended time for complicated assessment activities, we suggest the use of a simple Assessment of Speaking Skills Checklist (Table 7.2) in which the teacher records the oral language of individual students four times a year.

Table 7.2 Assessment of speaking skills checklist

Student name: _____		Grade: _____		
Indicator	Comprehension (understanding of oral academic conversations and classroom discussions)	Vocabulary (grade-level vocabulary in literature, social studies, science, mathematics)	Grammar (structure and organization of speech)	Fluency (fluent and effortless speech)
September	1 2 3 4	1 2 3 4	1 2 3 4	1 2 3 4
December	1 2 3 4	1 2 3 4	1 2 3 4	1 2 3 4
March	1 2 3 4	1 2 3 4	1 2 3 4	1 2 3 4
June	1 2 3 4	1 2 3 4	1 2 3 4	1 2 3 4

1 = *Not meeting grade level standards*   3 = *Meeting grade level standards*
2 = *Approaching grade level standards*   4 = *Beyond grade level standards*

Note: Ask your State Education Department or your School District for indicators to identify grade levels of oral language development

ASSESSING READING DEVELOPMENT AND PROFICIENCY

Students read for many purposes, and their reading involves the integration of their background knowledge, text structure, and reading strategies. In general, low-literacy students can understand simple material for informative purposes, and can understand the essential content of short, general, public statements and standard-ized messages. They can comprehend the ideas of simple informative materials written for native speakers, especially when these materials contain simple language structures and syntax, which rely on visual clues the readers have and some prior knowledge or experience with the topic. Students can often guess the meaning of unfamiliar words through use of cognates and text context. However, these students may have difficulties using higher-level cognitive skills such as in making inferences and drawing conclusions from text. They may have to read the material several times in order to fully capture the meaning.

Two important components in the development of reading skills with struggling ELL students are: (1) helping them to develop their own strategies in reading comprehension and, (2) providing them with the background knowledge needed to understand the conceptual and cultural framework of the assigned reading. Although assessment of reading should primarily focus on reading comprehension strategies (such as identification of the main ideas, conceptualization of the main points presented in the text, and the sequence of events in a story) struggling readers may not have developed these strategies and skills. One assessment strategy we recommend is observing how reading and writing develop in these students in order to identify their progress throughout their schooling years. Teachers will learn the most about their students' early reading development through their own observations. When observing the reading behaviors of strug-gling readers, teachers need to have in mind such questions as:

- Do students read literature that is appropriate to their grade level?
- Do students select and read a wide variety of materials?
- Do students participate in literature discussions?
- Are students able to read (at grade level) social studies/science textbooks?
- Can students read a science problem and follow the steps needed for its solution?
- Do students use reference materials independently?
- Do students interpret and expand meaning from literature and content area texts?

Observing students as they read silently provides us with more information about their reading characteristics or behaviors. Behaviors to be observed include: (1) students' level of concentration during sustained silent reading, (2) students' reluctance to stop reading when the period has ended, (3) spontaneous reaction during silent reading, (4) selection of reading materials of increasing difficulty, and (5) impatience with disturbances. Since reading comprehension is a matter of constructing meaning, the idea that students can read without comprehension makes no sense. The goal of observing the products of students' reading is to examine the meanings they construct:

- Do students make sense of what they have read?
- What are the meanings they construct?
- Do they integrate what they read with their background experiences?

The meanings students construct will vary and depend on their experiences. As we have said before, struggling ELLs have difficulty constructing meaning owing to variables such as: lack of conceptual background/prior knowledge, an over-dependence on one language system (e.g. graphophonemics), and/or an inability to integrate reading into their own experiences (Kucer, 2001).

For struggling ELLs, the *retelling inventory* is a good way of identifying students' strengths, as well as their reading deficiencies or needs. However, for upper elementary students, the piece of reading needs to be carefully chosen so that students do not feel that they are being treated as young children because they are ELLs and struggling in English literacy. In the *retelling inventory*, the teacher may ask a student to read a short story or a chapter in the social studies textbook, and retell a piece of information. Table 7.3 provides an example of a type of reading assessment task asked in a fourth-grade state assessment. Not only do teachers need to make

Table 7.3 Retelling inventory

The Cat	*Reading indicators*	*Acceptable*	*Emerging*
'Mom, why can't we get a cat?' I asked my mother.	retells accurate material presented in the text	X	
'I have told you already. Your father doesn't want a cat,' my mom tried to explain to me.	include information not stated explicitly		X
'Oh, please! Cant you convince him we need a cat?' I begged.	include information not stated implicitly or explicitly		X
'We don't need a cat, but I'll tell you what. I can't make any promises, but a lady I work with me has a cat who just had kittens and she's giving them away. Since your father's birthday is coming up, maybe we can get him	retelling the structure of the text		X
a kitten as a surprise so he won't know we got it until the cat is here. However, if he has a real problem with it, we will have to give the cat back.' My mom said.	provides background experience or knowledge of the understanding of the material	X	
'Yes! Thank you so much mom. Please talk to the lady tomorrow,' I said.			
I was so happy! I couldn't believe my mom was actually thinking about getting a cat. I	Uses details to retell major topics	X	
had been asking her for a while and every time, she told me my father didn't want a cat, but this time was different. She was thinking about it!	represent an adequate understanding of the text		X

Source: New York State Education Department (1998: 102)

students familiar with this type of assessment but it is also good to use it as a way of identifying information on students' reading progress. This inventory can be used continuously through the year to demonstrate a child's reading progress.

As we have discussed in earlier chapters, questioning plays an important role in schooling and in educating children. Answering questions is a common assessment strategy. Struggling ELLs have problems in answering questions at the end of the text or completing worksheets because they do not know how to go about the task of answering questions. Also, students who do not understand question asking and answering may experience difficulty in school because questions are a prominent feature in teachers' instruction and assessment. In using questions to assess reading comprehension, teachers need to develop a rubric or scale that identifies a maximum of three components to be assessed. For example, if a piece of literature is used, reading indicators may include: (1) identifying the concept or main idea presented, (2) describing the information source, and (3) listing important details, and level of interpretation of the text. Once the information of the rubric has been analyzed, teachers can start planning the appropriate instructional strategies. It has been found that successful readers often read the questions they are expected to answer before they read the text, even on standardized texts.

Another good assessment strategy is the analysis of reading miscues (Rhodes & Dudley-Marling, 1988). This can reveal students' strengths in graphophonemics, syntactic, semantic, and discourse knowledge. A careful analysis of students' miscues will help teachers gain a better understanding of students' reading process and behaviors: what students do when they read. A miscue is any oral reading response that does not match the text. Miscues follow a pattern and give educators information about readers' thought processes during reading, as in Table 7.4.

Although all students produce miscues when they read, good readers usually err on the meaning while struggling readers err on the structure of the language, especially on the side of phonics. Miscue analysis provides information on: (1) the

Table 7.4 Reading miscues

Example 1	There are big insects with large wings.
Reader 1	There are big insects with large *winds*. (a struggling reader) (semantically unacceptable)
Reader 2	There are big insects with *long* wings. (a successful reader) (semantically and syntactically acceptable)
Example 2	In his works, Ernest Hemingway portrayed characters who led daring and adventurous lives.
Reader 1	In his works, Ernest Hemingway *participated* characters who led daring and adventurous lives. (a struggling reader)
Reader 2	In his works, Ernest Hemingway *presented* characters who led daring and adventurous lives. (a successful reader)

reader's ability to use language and the reading process, and (2) the reader's approach to reading and reading comprehension.

In addition to the activities discussed in this chapter, there are several other activities that can be used to identify students' reading strengths and deficiencies. These are: reading logs, literature response journals, cloze tests, think aloud, and running records. All these assessment activities provide information that helps teachers to monitor students' progress.

ASSESSING ACADEMIC WRITING DEVELOPMENT AND PROFICIENCY

Academic writing consists mostly of mastered vocabulary, language structures, and well-organized content. When people write, they make choices about content and language (composition), and they also transcribe. They encode their meaning in print using the conventions of the English language. Transcription is the thinking of the words (Smith, 1971). Both of these two processes are important, but they require different strategies and different times. All too frequently, students' writing is evaluated in terms of transcription features such as punctuation, spelling, word usage, and grammar. Students' writing is also frequently evaluated using some formal test that examines their writing in terms of the presence or absence of these transcription features. However, for struggling ELLs, writing should be evaluated in terms of two general questions:

(1) Does the writing fulfill its purpose (to report, persuade, elicit feelings)?
(2) What do students know about writing, including writing conventions that help them to fulfill their purpose in writing?

Content, organization, and structure are three broad areas of writing that all students need to master at grade level. These areas include students' focus on central ideas within an organized and elaborated text, conveying meaning clearly and effectively and expressing ideas with appropriate grammar and structure. Teachers need to understand students' writing in order to assist them when planning instruction. For low-literacy-level students, the main writing emphasis should be on what they say (purpose, topic, and audience) and how they say it (language conventions).

Graves (1983) recommends that assessment of students' writing should be based on routine examination of their written work, including observing members of the whole class as they write. Graves also recommends spending about five minutes each day observing individual students. This observation involves the teacher sitting next to the students as they write, and Graves suggests that students are told of its purpose. Although struggling ELL students can express basic personal needs and compose short informal notes and messages on very familiar topics based on personal experiences, they often make major errors when expressing complex thoughts. Errors in spelling and grammar are frequent. We have observed that struggling ELLs have difficulties in expressing themselves in writing. Perhaps, this is because, in order to write appropriately, individuals need to stimulate higher-order thinking skills (such as the ability to make logical connections, to compare and contrast, and to generate solutions to problems) in order to support adequately an argument and its conclusions. Some teachers severely penalize students for spelling errors. Students who have had such teachers may regularly avoid the use of words they are not sure how to spell. They are reluctant to take chances with new words and, therefore, it may appear that these students have a limited writing vocabulary. In working with struggling readers, we have found that many students have not mastered the process of writing and, even if they are taught it, they have difficulties implementing it. What should teachers do with these students? We recommend that teachers provide sequential and continuous writing tasks to include process and products through:

- using open-ended tasks in which the student is asked to construct an essay either requiring or not requiring certain background knowledge;
- limiting the components of the writing process in the task (e.g. such as assigning a planning stage, or outlining, or even revising);
- writing short answers that may be an abbreviated check for a basic understanding of key points.

The literature on writing assessment suggests the use of the following assessment activities to monitor writing process and development: (1) learning logs, (2) writing surveys, (3) writing checklist, (4) writing prompts, and (5) peer assessment of writing. Learning logs provide opportunities for students to write in a variety of formats and topics. There are classrooms in which teachers ask students at the end of the day to indicate in the log what they learned. Looking at the writing of these students and commenting on their writing characteristics and comparing it over two or three months is a good way of assessing students' writing development. There are many writing checklists on the market, and most of them are useful in identifying students' writing progress. Our recommendation is for teachers to be consistent in using these checklists to inform students not only about their weakness, but also about their strengths. Showing students their progress in three months is a very successful way of motivating struggling writers to continue to use learning strategies in their writing. Writing prompts are useful in assessing students' acquired knowledge in any subject areas as well as for mirroring the thinking processes that students use during instruction. Table 7.5 provides writing prompts in mathematics, science, and social studies. Peer assessment of writing needs to be carefully organized to avoid fights among students. One way of implementing it is to provide students with a checklist to identify desirable indicators observed in the piece of writing assessed (e.g. uses periods and question marks correctly; writes in complete sentences; thoughts are organized). Again, teachers need to have a system for using this information in a systematic and objective way.

Table 7.5 Writing assessment prompts

Subject area	Prompt
Social studies	(1) Write a sentence about each of the following topics: (a) discrimination (b) ethnic diversity (2) There is a World Map in front of you. Identify a country you would like to visit and explain the reasons for visiting that country.
Science	(1) Describe the temperature yesterday and how you felt most of the time. (2) Today, you participated in an experiment showing that plants have chlorophyll. Describe the steps you follow to get to that conclusion.
Mathematics	(1) You have a problem in front of you. Explain how you would solve the problem. (2) Write a word problem similar to the one you described before.

MONITORING WRITING PROGRESS THROUGH A PORTFOLIO

We have found portfolio assessment to be a good way of monitoring the progress of struggling writers, and we recommend the use of a writing portfolio in assessing struggling ELLs. One of the advantages of using portfolio assessment is that it links assessment with instruction. That is, student performance is evaluated in relation to instructional goals, objectives and classroom activities. The three types of portfolios we recommend are: *The best work portfolio, Growth and learning portfolio* and the *English literacy development portfolio* (see Table 7.6).

The English literacy development portfolio includes pieces of writing from when the student started school up to pieces of writing at the current grade level. It also includes samples of work at the various stages of the writing process and writing products. For struggling readers, we suggest the teacher identifies the type of portfolio, and explains to students and parents the purpose for collecting these materials.

In addition to assessment portfolios, we have found that including rubrics or checklists of students' products provides a good overview of students' writing progress and development, overall linguistic and cognitive development in one or more areas of literacy. For example, if basic components of writing composition are the areas being assessed, a checklist may look like the one in Table 7.7.

At the end of the checklist there will be a statement focusing on the holistic scoring and indicating how well the composition as a whole accomplished the goal of the assignment. It will have criteria weighted using a point system (e.g. a 25-point scale). A monthly rubric should also be developed to transfer information from the

Table 7.6 Three types of portfolio

The best work portfolio
This is a selection of the best writing products in several writing categories such as: (1) compositions, (2) story summaries, (3) responses to literature, (4) content areas written tasks.
Growth and learning portfolio
This is a progress portfolio showing how students' writing has developed over a semester. It includes early drafts, rewrites, criticism of early work and an evaluation of how the writing has improved. Samples of students' work should be gathered because they provide exceptionally good evidence of student progress.
English literacy development portfolio
This includes several types of literacy products, and information about the characteristics of the student represented. We recommend an English literacy portfolio that includes several sections. The format can include: (1) profile of students' language, (2) literacy background knowledge, (3) writing process, and (4) writing products.

Table 7.7 Writing composition checklist

Indicator /Standard	Exemplary 4	Acceptable 3	Emerging 2	Unacceptable 1
The main idea, theme or point of view is clear and constantly maintained.				
Arguments and conclusions are adequately supported and explained.				
The logical flow of ideas are clear and connected.				
Spelling, grammar, punctuation are appropriate.				
Holistic scoring				
Overall evaluation:				

checklist to a more systematic rating. Teachers will then have detailed and rated information to be used as supplementary data to compare with the criterion-referenced and standardized testing information. The rubric will provide an overall impression of the elements of quality and levels of performance in a student's work. The scale usually ranges from a scale of 4 to 1, where 4 is the exemplary and 1 is unacceptable.

USING STANDARDIZED TEST DATA TO INFORM INSTRUCTION

Accountability is the responsibility of everyone involved in the education of students and plays an important role. Tests results are used to call school systems, educators and students to be publicly accountable and to demonstrate what students know, and what they are able to do. Fair accountability relies on appropriate and reliable assessment as a source of information that can be used together with other kinds of information (e.g. attendance, graduation rates) to make educational decisions about students' futures and to allocate support for students and schools. In doing so, there is a belief that public education should guarantee an equitable and excellent education for all students. More and more, politicians, educational policy makers, and educational administrators are pushing for standardized tools for identifying and comparing the educational achievement of students. The federal approach is to use testing as a mechanism for ensuring state and school district accountability based on clear and high standards and a system of annual assessment to measure students' progress against these standards.

High-stakes state tests have become the accountability tool of choice in many states as policy makers struggle to find ways to increase student achievement levels. The proponents of standards-based systemic reform maintain that, if high, rigorous standards are created for all students, and clearly communicated to educators, students, parents, policy makers, and the community at large, then a coordinated effort can be mounted that focuses on increased achievement. The expectation is that the academic performance of all students including English language learners will be increased and the entire system will be focused on helping students achieve those higher expectations. One way of getting this information is through the use of standardized assessment, which provides information on how students perform in relation to the average performance achieved by other students at the same grade level (i.e. the normative population). Educators are held accountable for the performance of their students on standardized tests. For the most part, there is a national agreement that there is a need for this type of assessment and that authentic measures are to be used by classroom teachers and schools in identifying individual progress based on a particular curriculum or set of individual standards.

States' assessments are usually based on states' curriculum frameworks or standards. The trend has been to make standards that are challenging to students rather than to limit them to minimum competencies or basic skills. When the school district or school is held accountable, testing occurs at certain grades: either grades

4, 8, and 11 or grades 3, 5 and 10. Individually, little is done with the results of these tests; they are used only to identify the grade level of students and the percentage of students in a particular school or district who are performing at grade level. Proponents of the use of standardized assessment recommend this type of assessment for the following reasons: (1) administration is speedy and efficient, (2) students' performance in a variety of skills can be measured, (3) data can be interpreted in relation to content and norms, and (4) students' scores can be compared with scores of other students. Educators need to objectively see these tests as providing information to add to the assessment information they have informally collected. These two kinds of information provide useful background for teaching and learning.

FACTORS TO CONSIDER IN EVALUATING ELLs ACHIEVEMENT THROUGH STANDARDIZED ASSESSMENT

The *No Child Left Behind* legislation (US Department of Education, 2001) requires school districts to provide programs with high academic standards. This legislation holds schools accountable for meeting annual measurement achievement objectives including making adequate yearly progress (AYP) for ELL students. No one doubts that, although the educational issues surrounding accountability are strong, often the assessment used does not reflect the diverse social, political, and economic characteristics and inequities of students (e.g. lack of resources, large class size, unsafe environments, inadequate funding, lack of technological resources, lack of English proficiency). For ethnically diverse groups, and especially for ELLs, standardized tests have broadened opportunities for quantitative analysis of the gaps in achievement between various ethnic and cultural groups. African Americans, Native Americans, and Hispanics, for example, have lagged significantly behind that of the general population. These groups, and especially those who are poor, are not reaching their academic potential. Disadvantages of these tests include:

(1)   they exclude important curriculum objectives;
(2)   they narrow the instructional focus;
(3)   they provide minimal information to guide instruction;
(4)   comparison of students with other students may not take into consideration their initial level within a continuum;
(5)   do not capture or reflect the diversity of the students' backgrounds and experiences.

In order to make assessment accountable or 'more fair' for ELLs, standardized data need to control factors such as: (1) level of English language proficiency, (2) prior formal school information, (3) length of time in the United States, and (4) type of home bilingual/English environment. If the 'accountable' data do not reflect the above factors, tests used for school and district accountability poorly serves the ELL school population since it does not present a holistic picture of the individual challenges, strengths and overall achievement of these students within a continuum.

However, because educators have no choice in deciding which tests are taken and who should take them, and because these assessments are here to stay, educators need to start making better use of these tests in the classrooms.

One of the crucial disadvantages is that standardized tests provide minimal information to guide instruction. Standardized tests are often administered in the spring semester, a few months before the end of the academic year. The answer sheets are then sent away for the test to be scored. By the time teachers receive students' results, several more weeks/months of the school year have gone by. Such circumstances work against the possibility of using the standardized tests for immediate instructional decisions. This is not to say, however, that educators should disregard the results and refuse to modify teaching plans if the results indicate otherwise.

Usually, these tests do not benefit struggling readers and writers at the instructional level because each test is guided by the attempt to sort and rank students in relation to one another rather than by an attempt to reflect what students actually know and can do. Because of the formats of some standardized English literacy assessments, they are also not effective in measuring higher-order thinking skills such as problem solving and drawing inferences. These tests emphasize discrete skills (Resnick and Klopfer, 1989). Because ELLs may not do well on these tests, schools may need additional accountability and assessment tools to measure ELLs' achievement. We recommend that the following data should be considered: (1) classes/courses taken and grades received, (2) graduation rates, (3) college attendance rates. Although these areas may not impact on the instructional decisions that teachers made for specific groups of students, the data will provide additional information on evaluating ELLs' long-term achievement in school and school districts.

Using Standardized Tests Results with ELLs

The words *standardized test* indicate that test administration, scoring of results and interpretations are done according to specific standards that include reference to a concept of 'normal'. When we use these tests we assume that the student's optimal performance is elicited, the results yield a valid measure of performance, and these tests supplement information known about children. Educators need to know the type of test and the purpose of the test: (1) to compare students with others of similar age, grade level, and/or (2) to identify the lists of skills or milestones markers that all children will presumably pass on their way to successful mastery of the developmental stage or academic subject. Teachers of ELLs need to be aware of state and local approaches toward assessment of this achievement, and to become thoroughly familiar with the multiple ways for documenting academic progress. Nitko (2001) suggests that appropriate use of the results of these tests can be helpful in:

- describing the educational developmental levels of each student;
- describing specific qualitative strengths and weakness in students;

- identifying the extent to which the student has attained the prerequisites needed to go into new or advanced learning;
- describing commonalities about students;
- describing students' performances with respect to specific targets;
- providing feedback to students about what kinds and levels of performances are expected of them;
- providing parents with feedback about students' progress toward learning goals.

The problem with standardized testing is that policy makers and educational agencies often rely exclusively on those tests to make decisions about teaching and instruction. The following list provides recommendations to schools on using standardized assessment data results in planning and delivering instruction.

Evaluate Relevance/Utility of Tests

Teachers need to evaluate the relevance and utility of standardized tests in the instructional history of ELLs. By reviewing the individual *profile of ELLs personal and cultural characteristics,* teachers identify the significance and usefulness of these tests relative to students' age, social and economic background, cultural background, level of English proficiency, and background in the English language, in addition to any other factor that the teachers consider relevant. Teachers then ask the question: Are these ELLs assumed to be 'normal' or are they at 'risk' by virtue of environmental, developmental, language or schooling factors? If the profile of personal and cultural characteristics indicates that ELL students are typical of other students tested, teachers need to use these test results to provide information for instruction. If the profile indicates the opposite, teachers need to make policy and decision makers aware that these students need other types of assessment and instruction that matches their personal, cultural, and language characteristics.

Assessment is Attached to Instruction

Appropriate use of these tests results may be helpful in verifying the student achievement level of a given grade level in the different subject areas, especially mathematics or reading. For example, if all fourth graders in a school district were given a standardized 'reading comprehension test' for the purpose of identifying the reading grade level, teachers might use the result of the test to identify which areas of reading comprehension are mastered by the struggling ELL, and how those results match with other assessment measures used by the teacher. If the analyses of both types of assessment yield the same conclusion, teachers can use this information to provide additional interventions to bridge the reading gap, so that these ELLs will be successful in the independent work required in fourth grade. In this example, the standardized test score is only part of the data used by the teacher to make instructional decisions about struggling ELLs.

Using the Standardized Test Result to Plan the Curriculum

The standardized test result may be useful in identifying academic areas and skills and to plan school and classroom curriculum. Usually, this step begins at the district level with what is called 'curriculum alignment,' and consists in identifying the overall academic areas based on an analysis of the information provided in a series of standardized tests that students are required to take. For example, a group of elementary school principals and fifth-grade teachers work with the district curriculum and reading coordinators to analyze the required state standardized test in English language arts. They use the information provided in selecting the reading to be included in the school district goals for literacy instruction. The curriculum for that particular district may include word attack skills, writing practices, and comprehension skills matching those identified in the test. Teachers can then also include those reading areas when they are working with struggling ELLs, perhaps at a lower level of emphasis but focusing on those reading areas identified by the school district as important components of the Literacy Program. Usually, this recommendation is not practiced by teachers of struggling ELLs; what we usually see is teachers compiling language and reading skills and materials without a specific literacy focus in mind.

Using the Standardized Test Results to Plan Individual Instruction

Standardized test information about students provides teachers with information to plan and individualize instruction. For example, in analyzing a struggling ELL who took the Comprehensive Test of Basic Skills (CTBS) test, it was found that in the section of vocabulary, Pedro (a struggling sixth grade student, reading at a second grade level) performs 'relatively' well in vocabulary identification, but extremely low in the area of reading comprehension. The recommended teaching approach is to use the strength of his 'adequate vocabulary' by teaching remedial literacy activities with interesting topics and enriched vocabulary with low level reading texts.

In summary, systematic procedure for using the results of a standardized achievement test to plan instruction for a group of struggling ELLs may include the following steps:

- review of ELLs' academic reports to determine weaknesses as well as strengths;
- establish instructional priorities;
- organize the group for instruction;
- plan instruction before beginning the instruction so that instructional students' targets and tasks are clearly identified;
- direct assessment of students' progress toward the instructional targets;
- carry out summative assessment on each student so that there is certainty that students have learned the identified targets and tasks.

CONCLUSION

Assessment is an integral part of the total academic picture of ELLs, and the information gathered through several strategies and tools provides the framework for appropriate diagnosis, effective instruction, and successful interventions. By definition, best practice dictates all decisions based on assessment information gleaned from multiple sources, and administrators and teachers need to find ways to match 'high stakes tests' with authentic assessment in order to better serve these ELL students. In addition, all the stake-holders in the care and education of ELLs (parents, teachers, and other related personnel) must be included in the process.

The most productive literacy assessment system for ELLs is one that provides information on the strengths and weakness of students in all language and literacy areas. This data needs to be analyzed from the perspective of the cultural and linguistic characteristics of ELLs so that they are not penalized for not scoring at grade level. On the contrary, this information should be used to provide resources, and interventions to improve instruction and learning. Although tests used for accountability purposes are necessary and important for comparing students, districts and schools, more emphasis should be given to the strengths identified in those tests and to using those results in scaffolding instruction to successful levels of academic development.

Developing Collaborative Literacy Relationships with Parents

Introduction

Parents' Influence on Children's Literacy Development and Achievement

Parents' Barriers to Effective School Involvement

Strategies for Parents' Involvement in their Children's Education

Improving Parents' Involvement Through Family Literacy Programs

Conclusion

CHAPTER 8

Developing Collaborative Literacy Relationships with Parents

Parents are natural advocates for their children, and yet may not know when and how to get involved. Schools need to view ethnically and linguistically diverse parents as concerned individuals who are able to contribute to the improvement of their children's progress. Recent education reforms by the US Department of Education such as *No Child Left Behind* (US Department of Education, 2001) stress the goal of parental participation in children's schooling. Many other educational policies – from site-based management to family support initiatives – emphasize building relationships with families, schools, and communities to promote children's academic success. The need for parental involvement is supported by compelling research evidence suggesting that parental involvement has positive effects on children's academic achievement (Bermudez & Marquez, 1996; Carrasquillo & London, 1993; Henderson, 1987; Shartrand *et al.*, 1997). The importance of family involvement grows out of convincing evidence of the strong contributions that families make to student achievement and school quality. When schools recognize the contributions that parents can make through school involvement, and work with these parents to support their children's learning, students tend to succeed not only in school but throughout life. Thus, parents are an important influence on children's academic development, and parents' involvement in literacy activities positively affects students' achievement. However, it is up to the school to develop a systematic plan for involving parents; they cannot wait for parents to initiate the collaboration with the school.

Family involvement efforts are most successful when teachers and schools assume that all parents want to do their best for their children and can make important contributions to their children's education. In addition, educators need to understand that there are barriers to parental involvement because of poverty, and financial and employment constraints. By taking an approach that identifies and builds on family strengths and resources, educators can build on this wealth of knowledge and skills to encourage participation from parents, especially those who may not seem to want to become involved.

This chapter provides an overview of how educators can help parents to become collaborators with schools in the academic development and advancement of ELLs who are struggling readers and writers. The first part of the chapter outlines the influential role of parents in the academic development of their children. The second part lists factors that can obstruct parental involvement, and offers an understanding of the challenges parents of ELL students face in their daily struggle to survive and raise their children. The third section identifies strategies that educators can implement to increase parental involvement and literacy development. The chapter ends by listing types of family literacy programs that educators can implement in schools where a significant number of ELLs are enrolled.

PARENTS' INFLUENCE ON CHILDREN'S LITERACY DEVELOPMENT AND ACHIEVEMENT

It is widely accepted that parental involvement has a positive influence on children's learning and literacy development. Schools, and especially teachers, should make special efforts to open communication with parents, encouraging them to take an active interest in their children's schoolwork and progress. Federal education programs and policies specify the involvement of families in their children's education. For instance, federal law (No Child Left Behind, US Department of Education. 2001) mandates that parents of special education students be involved in developing an Individual Educational Plan (IEP) with teachers and other school and professional personnel. Title I (ESEA, 2001) funds aimed at helping low-achieving children to meet challenging academic standards require schools to develop effective family involvement programs that include agreements of shared responsibility that are developed collaboratively with parents. These agreements describe school goals for student achievement, outline each stakeholder's role in achieving these goals, and require there be effective communication between school personnel and parents.

Since family involvement in education has positive effects on children's academic achievement, parents are a unique language resource for children and school. Schoolwork and homework become more rewarding when parents, teachers and administrators adopt strategies that support curriculum and academic goals. Parents can be influential in their children's development by: (1) becoming teachers of their children, (2) connecting themselves with their children' schools, (3) increasing their communication and collaboration with the school their children attend, and (4) establishing an effective home support for their children. Parental involvement is associated with numerous benefits to children, some of which are shown in Table 8.1.

Table 8.1 Some of the benefits of parental involvement

sustained gains in academic achievement;	enhanced English-language skills;
increased cognitive growth;	improved behaviors in school;
better home-school relationships;	more favorable attitudes toward school;
efforts to improve children's academic outcomes are more effective;	higher self-concept, much more effective;
fosters high students' achievement;	children do better in school;
children stay in school longer;	children go to better schools.

In addition, parents' active participation in their children's learning and schooling has long-term benefits. Among those:

- Efforts to improve children's academic outcomes are much more effective if families are directly involved in those efforts. The more parents know about what is going on in their children's schools, and the more active participants they become, the more effective they will be in helping their children to become successful learners.
- In general, children whose parents are constantly involved in their learning do better in school, and they stay in school longer than those children of uninvolved parents.
- Optimum academic performance occurs when the school, the parents, the whole family, and the students work together.

The literature (Carrasquillo & London, 1993; Cutler, 2000; Hoover-Dempsey & Sandler, 1995) repeatedly mentions that students do best when their parents are able to play four roles in their learning development: (1) role of teachers, (2) role of supporters, (3) role of advocates, and (4) role of decision-makers.

(1) **Role of teachers:** Parents play an active role in assessing their children's learning. Parents are s child's first language teachers. With every event that offers opportunities for meaningful communication, parents model ways of talking and interacting with the family. Through their actions and responses, parents help their child learn the language code, what to say to different audiences, and how to say it appropriately in a given situation.

(2) **Role of supporters:** The most accurate predictor of student achievement in school is the extent to which a family is able to: (a) create a home environment that encourages learning, (b) communicate high but reasonable expectations for the children's achievement and future careers, and (c) become involved in their children's education at home, at school and at the community (Henderson & Barla, 1995).

(3) **Role of advocates:** Parents are useful and instrumental in bringing change to

school programs in the curriculum, and in school status. Their advocacy efforts bring higher standards for teaching, learning, and academic achievement.

(4) **Role of decision-makers:** Parents can be instrumental in transforming a school from a 'high-needs school' to a 'high-achieving school.' Because parents are community members, their involvement and actions can bring change and better instructional opportunities for teachers and students.

Schools cannot work in isolation from students' families and the community. Rather, schools can benefit from parents' involvement in their children's education. Parents' involvement highly correlates with students' reading achievement (Henderson, 1987). Parents who participate in their children's education in school have an impact in becoming advocates for their children's education. For example:

- parents can increase their understanding of the school and their involvement in their children's education;
- parents can become more confident and vocal in their involvement with teachers;
- parents can show increased positive feelings about their roles as parents;
- parents can show more willingness to participate in school activities and to volunteer;
- parents increase their interactions with their children, with teachers, and with other school personnel, especially with the school principal.

Many parents of ELL students however, are not English-proficient themselves, and schools cannot expect these parents to help their children in a language they themselves have not mastered. However, parents are eager that their children should learn English. In some cases, because of their desire that their children learn English, parents are willing to 'sacrifice' their native language in the effort to direct/guide their children to acquire English skills as quickly as possible. This may lead parents to discourage the use of the native language in young children who have not yet reached verbal fluency. In such situations, the child may not achieve proficiency in either language, and will eventually become a struggling reader and writer. Schools need to provide guidance to parents to understand that what they need to encourage is their child's literacy development in the child's stronger language (English or native language). Parents need to know that once children become literate, they can transfer those skills of the native language into English with no difficulty. Table 8.4 provides a list of strategies teachers can recommend or initiate to help parents to promote language and literacy learning at home in the child's stronger language.

Parents need to be involved in the social, physical and academic development of their children. Parent–child time is a defining characteristic of parenting, and this is a good opportunity for parents and their children to do literacy-related activities together. These activities may be in the form of parents' reading to children from infancy through the upper grades. They can monitor their children's home reading and ask teachers to require regular reading homework. They can take children to the library and borrow or purchase books. Some parents of ELLs engage in these literacy activities during the early childhood years but, once students reach the fourth-grade level, parents begin to diminish their involvement. We recommend that parents do the opposite, and increase their involvement in literacy activities. Even if parents are not literate themselves, they should try to provide support and encouragement in their children's extra-curricular activities. Sometimes, identifying a tutor or an adult to sit with the child and the parent together is a good way of supporting and helping upper elementary ELL students.

PARENTS' BARRIERS TO EFFECTIVE SCHOOL INVOLVEMENT

Schools support parents by providing opportunities to strengthen parenting skills, enhance parent networks, and minimize the stress of parenting. Stressful circumstances can inhibit effective parenting practices, and as a result have negative effects on children's development and school achievement. Despite evidence of the positive educational effects of family involvement, parental involvement is still ignored by schools and parents alike. Schools do not systematically encourage family involvement and parents do not always participate when they are encouraged to do so. There are several major barriers to family/parent involvement in schools. Often, teachers deal with students and families challenged by poverty, single parenthood, low literacy, and lack of English language proficiency, and many other social demands. Such stressful circumstances can inhibit effective parenting practices and, as a result, have negative effects on children's development and school achievement. Although most parents of ELLs are interested in their children's well-being and school success, a significant percentage of these parents are more concerned with meeting their own immediate needs. Although schools cannot be responsible for meeting the needs of such families directly, they can learn to understand the connections between these challenges, social demands, family roles, and effective child-rearing practices.

Many parents of English language learners live in economic poverty, and increasingly, teachers deal with students and families challenged by such poverty. Economic poverty is also associated with numerous social challenges that affect children's readiness to learn, including health problems, crime-ridden neighborhoods, substandard housing, domestic violence, substance abuse, and family mobility as parents need to move to find work. Because of these shared conditions, behaviors and practices endemic to poor populations may be mistakenly labeled as cultural attributes of the parents of ELLs. As a result of this shared condition, behaviors and practices endemic to poor populations may be mistakenly labeled as cultural behaviors of parents. For example, the lack of reading skills among poor populations is sometimes attributed to an absence of 'value placed on literacy,' when in fact, economic constrains can severely limit parents' opportunity to view and interact with print of all kinds. Although teachers and school administrators are not responsible for meeting the needs of parents, they can learn to understand the connections that exist between poverty, family functioning, and children.

Changing demographics and employment patterns may further complicate the development of strong home partnerships. Many of these parents work, and cannot assist teachers in the classroom. Therefore, their involvement needs to be seen in the form of supporting what teachers do with the children and not necessarily through their presence at school. In many schools, parental involvement is still measured by parents' presence through school hours. How many schools organize meetings on Sundays when a significant number of parents are not working? How many schools plan to call parents between 9:00 and 10:00 PM when these parents are home and are able and willing to receive a 'friendly' call from their child's school?

As the population becomes increasingly diverse, parents will likely come from different cultural and economic backgrounds, leading to constraints in their involvement in their children's education. Family structure is associated with children's early literacy activities and early school problems. A significant number of parents of ELL students are single parents. Children in single-parent families are more likely to experience early school problems, and are less likely to participate in early literacy activities than children in two-parent families. In addition, many of these single parents need to hold two jobs in order to be able to meet the economic demands of the family. This fact has a tremendous impact on family and it affects family involvement in children's education because this double-employment pattern gives parents less time to spend on school related activities.

There are parents who do not speak English, the language of the school. Parents may feel 'deprived' when they go to the school and are confronted by a group of English-speaking educators. They may even feel 'ashamed' because they do not speak the language of the school. In addition, some parents may even exhibit cultural traits that are different from those of the teachers of their children and may uphold values that appear to clash with mainstream US practices and beliefs about education and family roles. For example, the desire to learn English is a powerful incentive for most parents of ELL students. However, parents whose English is limited should not be discouraged from participating in their children's education. Schools should have a systematic plan to involve parents who are not English speakers. Usually, schools have temporary plans based on federally-funded programs or community initiatives, but these temporary plans are not acceptable if schools want to maintain parent–school relationships.

Another barrier to family involvement in children's schooling is the negative attitude towards family involvement commonly held by both teachers and parents. Teachers often believe that parents are neither interested in participating in their children's education, nor qualified to do so. Parents sometimes feel intimidated by school administrators and teachers and feel that they lack the knowledge and skills to help educate their children. Teachers often lack the confidence to work closely with parents of language-minority students. Because many of the teachers do not speak the language of the parents, they feel concern about the level of communication they are able to have with these parents. Some of the immigrant parents come from countries where teachers are more authoritarian that those in the US, and learning is not seen as a participatory process. As a result, they may feel ill at ease with pedagogical practices that encourage them to take responsibility for their own learning. Similarly, parents may be reluctant to become actively involved in their children's schooling because they view such involvement as an improper challenge to the authority of the teacher and the school.

Many parents feel uncomfortable engaging in school-related activities without an invitation and guidance from the teacher of their children. Teachers need to be aware that parents wait for that invitation to become active participants. Through this approach of inviting parents, teachers can provide parents with special strategies to increase the value of home reading, such as talking to children about the characteristics of the main characters and plots of a particular story already read by the child, and asking them to make predictions, or else to summarize stories on children's books. Parents can serve as volunteer listeners or tutors in school. Perhaps, most importantly, parents can communicate love of reading, pleasure in their children's reading progress, and support for the school's efforts to ensure literacy of all children. Also, parents can advocate within the school and beyond, for the use of effective instructional reading methods for all. Likewise, parents can inform teachers about children's reading and writing experiences, and can collaborate in supporting teachers' instructional strategies.

STRATEGIES FOR PARENTS' INVOLVEMENT IN THEIR CHILDREN'S EDUCATION

Parents of struggling readers and writers are perhaps the ones who need the most assistance in helping their children in school-related tasks. Teachers need to communicate with parents and to tell them that both the teacher and the parent are working together for a common goal, which is to improve their child's literacy skills. Some families may come from a culture with no tradition of parents playing an active role in their children's education. Therefore, educators need to be sensitive to these parents' view of schooling, and work around those views to help parents and children at the same time. The following activities are recommended as initial strategies to provide parents of struggling readers and writers with structured and scheduled tasks. Although educators do not have to implement all these strategies at the same time, we recommend initially, that teachers try out as many of these activities as they can in order to involve the parents and make them aware that their children need support from school and from home in order to become successful readers and writers.

Information on Yearly Subject Areas' Academic Requirements

We recommend that parents be given specific information on what is needed on a yearly basis for the child to accomplish in order to do satisfactory grade level work.

Initially, we recommend that information be given in only two subject areas (English language arts and mathematics) so as not to overwhelm the parent. These two subject areas are literacy-related and are important areas in which achievement is needed to meet grade-level academic standards. Information is given to parents in advance, on the specific educational skills and tasks their child needs to fulfill in the areas of language arts (reading and writing) and mathematics in order to satis-factorily complete work for that grade level.

Parents should be informed that, if their children are not able to perform these tasks at the end of the year, then, there is the possibility that the children may not be promoted to the next grade level. This is not a threat, but a specific invitation for parents to help their children. For parents of struggling readers, it is not enough to send parents 'homework' or 'daily tasks', they should be informed, in writing and in person, of what the child must master on a yearly basis in each subject area. We have found that informing parents (in both languages) of ELLs through a short list of 'what the child is expected to know' helps the parents to understand their chil-dren's expected/required academic tasks by subject areas. In this way, the school is telling parents that their help is needed in helping children to succeed. Table 8.2 presents an example of a short list that a school may send to parents during the first month of the academic year to tell them what they need to know about mathematics for fourth-grade students. In this way, when daily homework is sent, parents will remember the bigger picture and feel obligated to include mathematics in some of their daily literacy home tasks in helping children to succeed in fourth grade.

Once the short list is sent to parents, the school should make every effort to help them understand these concepts and to help them to 'commit themselves' to identifying how they are going to help their children to pass/acquire those skills. We have found that, once those parents see the bigger picture, their role may be more practical and effective.

Table 8.2 What your fourth grade child needs to be able to do in mathematics

use logical reasoning to solve simple mathematics problems;
use logical reasoning to develop mathematical conclusions;
compare and describe quantities, express relationships and relate mathematics to the immediate environment;
identify patterns in a number sequence;
explain and solve mathematics problems using addition, subtraction, multiplication and subtraction processes;
use simple algebraic expressions to describe and compare quantities;
use simple geometric that summarize information;
identify patterns in a number sequence;
estimate and measure surface areas.

Monthly Workshops

Effective schools provide monthly workshops for parents with the purpose of updating parents and families as to what is going on in their children's school and informing them about general educational issues relevant to their children's academic achievement. These meetings need to be scheduled ahead of time, with an invitation sent to parents at the beginning of the school year and again one or two weeks before the activity is held. Telephone call reminders are also recommended. If parents cannot be reached via telephone, a voice-mail message on their home telephone is always a good reminder. Table 8.3 lists suggested topics for those monthly meetings.

Educators need to recognize that some of these parents may not be accustomed to visiting the school throughout the year. If their child is well behaved and doing well in school, parents see no reason to visit the school. Monthly workshops need to be perceived as parent–teacher friendly, where teachers are learning from parents and parents are learning from teachers. We have attended monthly meetings that have included a 'parent must do' list in which a school authority, usually the school principal, describes the list, and gives a copy to parents. However, parents did not have an opportunity to add to the list. This approach, rather than motivating parents to become involved in their children's literature development, helps to distance parents from school since they may perceive the approach as a reprimand rather than as a useful recommendation in increasing their children's academic development. School and teachers should prepare materials carefully for these monthly meetings and, if possible, provide opportunities for parents to collaborate in the planning and implementation of these meetings and strategies. Perhaps every month, a parent can be identified who would demonstrate/illustrate one or two of the recommended literacy strategies.

Table 8.3 Topics for monthly meetings

Stages of child development.
Children's motivation and self esteem.
First and second language development.
Children's growth and parenting.
Increasing school and parent participation in the academic future of children.
Communication and parenting.
The school reading and writing program.
What your child should know at the end of the school year.
The mathematics fourth grade (fifth/sixth grade) program.
Suggested reading and writing activities that parents can use at home with upper elementary children.
Extracurricular reading and writing activities for fourth grade (fifth/sixth grade) students.

Homework Assistance

Homework is essential for practicing and applying the skills taught in school. Unfortunately, many parents and other family members, especially those who speak a language other than English, feel 'ill-equipped' to assist their children with homework. Teachers' initial communication with parents should encourage and invite (rather than demand) them to get involved in their children's education. Encouraging messages and letters are sent to parents inviting them to check their child's homework every evening/night and sign off on it. Checking homework at home may be something parents have never been asked to do before. And, although the strategy of signing off may prove stressful to parents who do not want to sign off on material they do not understand and may be confusing, teachers can reinforce this practice until parents see the need to be accountable for their children's homework. Perhaps, the initial communication is an 'invitation' to parents to check homework daily for 'neatness,' legibility' and 'completion.' Later on, parents can be asked to check homework for content literacy and for development of additional reading and writing skills.

In addition to helping the child with homework, teachers can find ways to invite parents to go work with their children in home literacy activities. Table 8.4 lists several activities that parents can be trained to do with their children at home.

The last activity in Table 8.4 (that of turning off the TV at a determined time every day so that every family member can accomplish a literacy activity) is highly recommended. Family literacy activities may include reading the newspaper (in English

Table 8.4 Ways that parents can promote literacy at home

Reading to their children as early and as often as possible. This reading can be done in English or in the native language.
Making a habit of visiting the public/community library to choose books for their children and for themselves.
Having a book center/corner (books, newspapers, magazines, comic strips) in an assigned place at home. This does not have to be a big space; it can even be in the kitchen, if no other space is available.
Becoming familiar, through the community newspaper, with educational activities in the community (e.g. puppet shows, zoo presentations, libraries educational programs) and making these activities part of the monthly/weekly parent child educational schedule.
Practicing oral stories with children, even if this is done in the native language.
Talking to the children and listening to their stories. Parents should engage children in meaningful conversations.
Providing children's opportunities to write (e.g. letters to relatives, leaving a written message for children that requires a written response).
Identifying a specific time for the parent and the child to read together. TV should be off and, at that time, every member of the family should be involved in an educational/literacy activity.

or in the family's native language), looking through a magazine, writing a letter to a relative, paying monthly bills, reading a book, or working on the computer. By doing these literacy activities together, parents are showing their children that literacy time is an important event in the daily life of all the members of the family. What we have commonly seen is parents asking their children to do homework while the parents continue watching TV in the same room that their children are doing the academic tasks. This behavior is unacceptable since it sends a negative message to the child related to his/her literacy development/schooling as being ignored by his/her parents.

Individual Meetings with Parents

For those struggling upper elementary ELL students, teachers need to arrange interviews and meetings with the parents on an on-going basis. These meetings should be held in school, preferably in the teacher's classroom so that teachers can show parents the materials and textbooks that the students are using, as well as the child's work, and test results. Teachers need to use encouraging strategies, even if the child is not showing academic growth. One way to do this is to begin by sending home a personal letter inviting parents to attend a meeting to share information about the child. The invitation letter may look like this one.

Dear Ms Ramona Serrano:

My name is Ms Rossana Robinson and I am the teacher of your daughter Kenia Martinez. I am very happy to have your daughter Kenia in my class 4-A (Room 301). And, it is in your child's best interest that you and I work together on her academic progress.

I would like to meet with you so that I can get to know your child better. I also would like to tell you what is expected of Kenia at the end of this semester and at the end of the academic year.

I am inviting you to meet with me on Monday, September 29 at 10:00 AM in my classroom (Room 301). If you cannot meet with me on September 29, please let me know when is the best day and time to meet with me. I am available to meet with you at a time which is convenient to you and me.

Sincerely,
Rosanna Robinson,
Fourth Grade Teacher, Room 301, PS 30

But teachers do not begin sharing information about the academic difficulties with parents at this first meeting. Rather, they emphasize what is expected from the child at the end of the academic year, explaining how the parent can reinforce the teacher's work by working at home with the child. Once the parent is motivated to work with the teacher, a follow-up meeting may include informing the parent of areas of academic development where the child is performing poorly, and then the teacher can offer specific strategies for the parents to implement at home. We have found that these monthly meetings are very useful with parents of struggling readers and writers. Parents feel that the school is really making an effort to reach every child. However, we do understand that these individual meetings put another layer of responsibility on the teacher. Perhaps, teachers need additional time during the day to plan and implement this activity. But if it is true that everyone is interested in helping struggling readers and writers, the school and the school district need to provide the necessary resources to the classroom teacher to accomplish these tasks.

The Use of the Home Language

Parents need to be told that the use of the home language, even if that language is not English, is an effective tool during the family literacy activities. Using the home language allows parents to pass on cultural concepts and literacy skills that enhance learning and in the long run, contributes to the acquisition of English. Recommendations to parents where they can use the home language is a strategy of the school that shows/demonstrates respect for parents' culture and the recognition of the benefits of becoming bilingual. Although parents should be encouraged to learn English, a recommended strategy is to use the parents' language in school for meetings or other parent-related activities. The use of the home language is an effective tool for parent involvement activities. Using the home language at school allows school personnel to convey abstract parenting and cultural concepts, to develop literacy skills that enhance acquisition of English, and also show acceptance of parents and the community linguistic and cultural background.

Integrating Parents Feedback into the Curriculum.

Schools should develop strategies to encourage parents' ongoing feedback on school issues. For example, schools should consider including parents in decisions about issues ranging from schedule to the content of the curriculum. We suggest that curriculum developers should draw on parents' knowledge and experiences to integrate salient cultural interests and social issues into literacy content. Another strategy we have seen implemented is the use of a short survey or questionnaire (translated into the parents/community language) asking parents for opinions on certain school activities or programs. For example, if a new reading program is going to be implemented, the school can send parents a brief description of the new program and ask them to comment on this new innovative instructional activity. And, even if few parents answer the questionnaire, the schools have demonstrated an interest in receiving parents' feedback. The school can then take a further step and invite parents to school to explain the program, the students' challenges and parents' involvement in this endeavor.

IMPROVING PARENTS' INVOLVEMENT THROUGH FAMILY LITERACY PROGRAMS

There is a need to develop positive relationships between parents and schools. As said before, for many parents of ELLs, the desire to help their children is there; however, the parents themselves often do not have the literacy skills to help their children. One approach to help parents become familiar with literature or literacy is through family literacy programs. All these programs draw school and parents closer for the benefit of children and youth. The opportunity to learn provides a powerful motivation for parents to participate in family literacy programs, especially when offered in environments that are less threatening than those of other formal courses available to adults. Usually, parents of struggling readers and writers are the ones who probably benefit the most by participating in these literacy programs. By participating in these programs, parents see themselves as becoming active in family literacy programs and learners themselves. Parents can then be better 'equipped' to identify themselves with the learning challenges of their children and be more at ease to help their children at home. The following recommendations offer ideas for realistic family literacy programs in which we have seen parents of English language learners become interested in participating in order to help their children to be successful learners.

Literacy Programs

For parents of ELLs who are not themselves fully literate, it is especially critical to have meaningful opportunities to enhance their own literacy skills. Schools need to strengthen family literacy programs and encourage parents to participate in various ways, such as learning how to read and write, and stressing parent–child learning strategies (e.g. reading/writing activities, English as a second language through practical activities, development of literacy skills in the native language). For non-English-speaking parents, literacy programs work better when they are offered in the parents' native language.

One of the authors worked with New York State Mount Vernon Public Schools which, in collaboration with the Westchester Jewish Community Services Center and Fordham University, designed two adult literacy education training models to prepare parents to read to their children and to provide them with strategies to help their children improve their reading skills. Recognizing that parents' literacy skills have an immense impact on children's academic achievement, the project provided adult literacy programming for those parents who lacked adequate reading skills. Two adult literacy models were provided: (1) parents alone attended literacy skills training, (2) parents and their children together attended an after-school program where literacy activities were geared at parents working with students in reading related activities. In addition, in both groups, books were distributed to participating parents and children. Both programs integrated children's literature into the training. Parents received 15 hours of training through an academic semester, followed up with meetings the next academic semester, where they talked and described the parent-child interactive sessions. At the end of the project, students' academic data indicated that students whose parents attended/participated in these literacy programs showed increased scores in English language arts, especially in the area of reading.

English as a Second Language Programs

Schools should encourage parents to learn English as a strategy to better help their children at home. English as a second language (ESL) programs should be implemented in the school or in collaboration with community agencies to help parents become familiar with the language of the school. Programs should be flexible enough to allow working parents to be part of such programs. Most ESL programs we have seen are offered only during school hours to accommodate those parents who do not work and who bring their children to school in the morning and can stay for the literacy class. Perhaps an alternative program can be organized with a community center or the community library to offer classes during the evenings or during the weekends. The Mount Vernon model described above may be a good approach to implement for parents to learn English. A recommendation to follow is not to concentrate so much on oral development but more on the reading and writing components. Adults are very sensitive toward their spoken language, and many non-English-speaking parents may not welcome a program whose main focus is on the oral development of adults. Whatever the focus of the program, it needs to be related to strategies that parents can use with their children.

Another recommendation to follow is to give parents incentives to remain in the program. A resource to be consider is 'baby sitting,' since many parents of these children do not have the financial resources to pay for baby sitting while they are attending these classes. Personal observations indicate that, initially, these programs are very well attended. However, after the first six sessions, attendance decreases to less than 50% of the adults who registered for the program. We think that, if the program is designed and implemented around parents' interests in helping their children with English-related tasks, parents will be more willing to participate and stay in these adult ESL programs.

Computer Literacy Programs

Recently, adults have been very much interested in learning how to operate computers. Today, computers are found in many homes, and children make use of computers for game-related activities. However, although these homes may have computers, few parents make use of them. Personal observations of how parents of ELLs feel about these computers is that they feel threatened by them, sometimes because of their own lack of English skills. Therefore, computer literacy programs can play an important role in the academic development of parents: (1) to develop computer literacy, (2) to develop English literacy, (3) to use the computer to learn concepts and skills, and (4) to help their children at home, using the computer as a learning tool. For example, parents may learn how to use the word processor to write simple letters, and how to use the Internet to get information about topics in the different subject areas that are part of their children's school curriculum. Computers are also useful in completing home literacy tasks and homework.

We understand that computer literacy programs are expensive to operate, but the school can develop partnerships with computer companies and community centers to implement these programs. If these programs are well-developed and the instructors understand the strengths and needs of the parents, these programs are successful in achieving the goals indicated above.

Native Language Literature Programs

In addition to promoting cultural respect and making parents of ELLs more comfortable in family-literacy projects, native language literature programs help schools to establish a collection of native language materials for the use of parents, children, or staff. This approach is an additional creative way of involving parents in literacy activities. Parents can participate in this program by bringing books, by suggesting titles and by providing reasons for the inclusion of these books. They may even be able to write a simple synopsis of the book. We have observed that, when parents feel that their language and culture is valued by the school and its teachers, they are motivated to participate. The model emphasizes that the school is learning from the parents, and that parents are the main contributors to this program. Perhaps the 'School Parents Association' can identified funds available to parents who may know of a book but do not have the money to buy it. A room needs to be available for this project, and the school needs to identify a resource individual to work in the project. This resource person should be compensated for time spent working with the parents so that activities are planned and implemented throughout the academic year. This resource person is also accountable to the program success. An ongoing project like this, if it is well coordinated and presented, allows adults who are not literate in their own language to develop literacy skills, and encourages adults to continue using their native language during family literacy activities with their children. The school can seek funding for the project through small grants or community organizations.

CONCLUSION

Developing collaborative relationships between schools and parents is a two-way communication effort. This relationship can sometimes be difficult because of the many challenges faced by many schools and many parents. It is not always a question of who is responsible, or if parents or teachers should be more involved with the responsibility of educating ELLs. We may argue that schooling is the role of the school, and that this is the reason why the government has in its budget a significant amount of money for providing personnel who are specialized in educating children and youth. Others may recommend that, although the government has schools, schools can do only so much, and that it is ultimately the responsibility of the parents to follow up at home what the school has introduced on a given day or week. It is the authors' opinion that it is the responsibility of educators as well as parents/guardians to support one another in the role of nurturing and educating ELLs. That is the reason that this chapter provided strategies for educators and parents to best collaborate in this important role.

The challenges inherent in working with a diverse community can be transformed into enrichment when both sides value involvement and provide the time and resources to work toward shared goals of academic and social achievement of the children/students. This school/parent partnership centers on identifying common goals and working together in reciprocal support that demonstrates and understands that it is a two-way relationship.

Resources for Teachers of ELL Students

INSTRUCTIONAL STRATEGIES

Brisk, M.E. and Harrington, M.M. (2002) *Literacy and Bilingualism: A Handbook for All Teachers.* Mahwah, NJ: Lawrence Erlbaum.

Chamot, A.U., O'Malley, J.M., Chamot, E. and Sista, C. (1994) *CALLA Handbook: Implementing the Cognitive Academic Language Learning.* Reading, MA: Addison-Wesley

Herrell, A. and Jordan, M. (2004) *Fifty Strategies for Teaching English Language Learners* (2nd edn). Upper Saddle River, NJ: Merrill Prentice Hall.

Oxford, R.L. (1990) *Language Learning Strategies. What Every Teacher Should Know.* New York: Newbury.

Peregoy, S.F. and Boyle, O.F. (2001) *Reading, Writing, and Learning in ESL: A Resource Book for K-12 Teachers* (3rd edn). New York: Longman.

Schecter, S.R. and Cummins, J. (2003) *Multilingual Education in Practice. Using Diversity as a Resource.* Portsmouth, NH: Heinemann

Tiedt, P.L. and Tiedt, I.M. (1995) *Multicultural Teaching: A Handbook of Activities, Information, and Resources* (4th edn). Boston, MA: Allyn and Bacon.

Tompkins, G.E. (2004) *Fifty Literacy Strategies: Step by Step* (2nd edn). Upper Saddle River, NJ: Merrill Prentice Hall.

WEBSITES PROVIDING INFORMATION ON ESL AND ENGLISH LANGUAGE ARTS

ESL lessons:
    http://members.aol.com/Jakajk/ESLLessons.html
Links to other ESL websites are posted on:
    http://www.eslgames.com/
Dave's ESL café:
    http://www.eslcafe.com/
Offers lesson ideas, games, software, and much more:
    http://esl.about.com/index.htm
Teachers helping teachers:
    http://www.pacificnet.net/~mandel/LanguageArts.html

TESOL journal; offers teaching techniques, ideas and articles:
http://www.aitech.ac.jp/~iteslj/
Language arts lesson plans:
http://www.col-ed.org/cur/lang.html,
http://ericir.syr.edu/Virtual/Lessons
http://www.education-world.com
Lessons in all content areas and grades:
http://www.lessonsplanspage.com
English as a Second Language World Wide Web Sites (EWU Libraries Guide). Links to other
ESL sites are available:
http://www.library.ewu.edu/help/selectedresources/wwwesl.html
Content and standards based lessons:
http://www.wcom.com/marcopolo/
Strategies for enhancing learning:
http://www.ncret.org/tandl/impleml.htm
Web 66: A K-12 World Wide Web project:
http://web66.coled.umn.edu
Balanced literacy:
http://www.rigby.com
Diversity:
http://execpc.com/~dboals/diversity.html
The Web of Culture:
http://www.worldculture.com
The Technology and Learning Center for Teachers:
http://www.nationalteacher.org
Publications on using technology for language teaching:
http://www.ruthvilmi.net/hut/Publication/international.html
Teaching English to speakers of other languages:
http://www.tesol.org
Center for Applied Linguistics
http://www.cal.org
The National Research Center on English Learning and Achievement:
http://cela.albany.edu/
Center for Research on Education, Diversity and Excellence:
http://www.crede.ucsc.edu/
The American Association for Applied Linguistics:
http://www.aaal.org/
US Department of Education:
http://www.ed.gov/
National Board Association, Education Trends and Tools:
http://www.nsba.org/itte/
Education Daily:
http://www.educationdaily.com
Lesson plans:
http://www.csun.edu

References

Allington, R.L. and Walmsley, S.A. (1995) *No Quick Fix: Rethinking Literacy Programs in America's Schools*. Newark, DE: International Reading Association.

Alvermann, D. and Phelps, S. (1998) *Content Reading and Literacy: Succeeding in Today's Diverse Classrooms*. Boston, MA: Allyn & Bacon.

Alvermann, D. and Ridgeway, V. (1990) Implementing content area reading with limited finances. In G. Duffy (ed.) *Reading The Elementary School* (pp. 200–208). Newark, DE: International Reading Association.

Alvermann, D. and Swarford, J. (1989) Do content area strategies have a research base? *Journal of Reading* 32, 388–394.

Anno, M. (1999) *Anno's Math Games*. New York: Bt. Bound, Philomel Books.

Baker, C. (2001) *Foundations of Bilingual Education and Bilingualism* (3rd edn). Clevedon: Multilingual Matters.

Baker, L. and Brown, A.L. (1984) Metacognitive skills and reading. In P.D. Pearson, R. Barr, M.L. Kamil and P. Mosenthal (eds) *Handbook of Reading Research*. New York: Longman.

Baker, C. and Prys Jones, S. (1998) *Encyclopedia of Bilingualism and Bilingual Education*. Clevedon: Multilingual Matters.

Bermudez, A. and Marquez, J. (1996) An examination of a four-way collaborative to increase parental involvement in the schools. *The Journal of Educational Issues of Minority Students* 16 (summer), 1–16.

Bernhardt, E.B. (2000) Second-language reading as a case study of reading scholarship in the 20th century. In M. Kamil, P. Mosenthal, P.D. Pearson and R. Barr (eds) *Handbook of Reading Research* (Vol. 3: pp. 813–834). Mahwah, NJ: Erlbaum.

Bernhardt, E.B. and Kamil, M.L. (1995) Interpreting relationships between L1 and L2 reading: Consolidating the linguistic threshold and the linguistic interdependence hypotheses. *Applied Linguistics* 16 (1), 15–34.

Bilingual Education Act (1967) S. 428, 90th Congress, 1st session.

Bruner, J. (1974) The ontogenesis of speech acts. *Journal of Child Language* 2, 1–19.

Burns, M. (1992) *About Teaching Mathematics: A K–8 Resource*. Sausalito, CA: Math Solutions Publications.

Bunting, E. (1988) *How Many Days to America? A Thanksgiving Story*. Boston, MA: Houghton Mifflin.

Carrasquillo. A.L. (1994) *Teaching English as a Second Language: A Resource Guide*. New York: Garland Publishing.

Carrasquillo, A. and London, C. (1993) *Parents and Schools*. New York: Garland.

Carrasquillo, A. and Rodriguez, V. (2002) *Language Minority Students in the Mainstream Classroom*. Clevedon: Multilingual Matters.

Clegg, J. (ed.) (1996) *Mainstreaming ESL: Case Studies in Integrating ESL Students into the Mainstream Curriculum*. Clevedon: Multilingual Matters.

Cohen, A.D. (1994) *Assessing Language Ability in the Classroom*. Boston, MA: Heinle and Heinle.

Cooper, J.D. with Kiger, N.D. (2003) *Literacy: Helping Children Construct Meaning* (5th edn). New York: Houghton Mifflin.

Cummins, J. (1980) The construct of language proficiency in bilingual education. In J.E. Alatis (ed.) *Georgetown University Roundtable on Languages and Linguistics* (pp. 76–93). Washington DC: Georgetown University Press.

Cummins, J. (1994) The acquisition of English as a second language. In K. Spangenberg-Urbschat and R. Pritchard (eds) *Kids Come in All Languages: Reading Instruction for ESL Students* (pp. 36–62). Newark, DE: International Reading Association.

Cummins, J. (2001) *Language, Power, and Pedagogy: Bilingual Children in the Crossfire*. Clevedon: Multilingual Matters.

Cummins, J. (2002) *Language, Power and Pedagogy*. Clevedon: Multilingual Matters.

Cutler, W.W. (2000) *Parents and Schools: The 150 Years Struggle for Control in American Education*. Chicago, IL: University of Chicago Press.

Darling-Hammond, L. (1994) Performance-based assessment and educational equity. *Harvard Educational Review* 53, 5–30.

De Avila, E. (1997) Setting expected gains for non and limited English proficient students. *NCBE Resource Collection Series No. 8*. Washington, DC: National Clearinghouse Bilingual Education.

Diamond, B.J. and Moore, M.M. (1995) *Multicultural Literacy: Mirroring the Reality of the Classroom*. White Plains, NY: Longman.

Dulay, H. and Burt, M. (1977) Remarks on creativity in language acquisition. In M. Burt, H. Dulay and M. Finochiarro (eds) *Viewpoints on English as a Second Language*. New York: Regents.

Echeverrria, J. and Graves, A. (1999) *Sheltered Content Instruction: Teaching English-language Learners with Diverse Abilities*. Boston, MA: Allyn & Bacon.

Edelsky, C. (1986) *Writing in a Bilingual Program*. Norwood, NJ: Ablex.

ESEA (2001) *Elementary and Secondary Education Act*. Washington, DC: Government Printing Office.

Fathman, A.K., Quinn, M.E. and Kessler, C. (1992) *Teaching Science to English Learner, Grades 4–8*. Washington, DC: National Clearinghouse for Bilingual Education.

Fitzgerald, J. (1993) Literacy and students who are learning English as a second language. *The Reading Teacher* 46, 638–647.

Fitzgerald, J. (1995) English-as-a-second language learners' cognitive reading processes: A review of research in the United States. *Review of Educational Research* 65, 145–190.

Fountas, I.C. and Pinnell, G.S. (2001) *Guiding Readers and Writers Grades 3–6: Teaching Comprehension, Genre, and Content Literacy*. Portsmouth, NH: Heinemann.

Freeman, D. and Freeman, Y. (1994) *Between Worlds: Access to Second Language Acquisition*. Portsmouth, NH: Heinemann.

Freeman, D.E. and Freeman, Y.S. (2001) *Between Worlds: Access to Second Language Acquisition* (2nd edn). Portsmouth, NH: Heinemann.

Freeman, Y.S. and Freeman, D.E. (2002) *Closing the Achievement Gap: How to Reach Limited-formal-schooling and Long-term English Learners*. Portsmouth, NH: Heinemann.

GAO (2001) *Meeting the Needs of Students with Limited English Proficiency*. Washington, DC: United States General Accounting Office.

Garcia, G.E. (2000) Bilingual children's reading. In M. Kamil, P. Mosenthal, P.D. Pearson and R. Barr (eds) *Handbook of Reading Research* (Vol. 3; pp. 813–834). Mahwah, NJ: Erlbaum.

Garcia, G. (1992) Linguistically and culturally diverse children: Effective instructional practices and related policy issues. In H.C. Waxman, J. Walker de Felix, J.W. Anderson and H.P. Baptise Jr (eds) *Students in At-risk Schools: Improving Environments for Learning* (pp. 65–86). Thousand Oaks, CA: Corwin.

Genesee, F. (1989) Early bilingual development: One language or two? *Journal of Child Language* 16, 161–179.

Gersten, R. (1996) Literacy instruction for language-minority students: The transition years. *The Elementary School Journal* 96, 227–244.

Goldenberg, C. (1996) The education of language-minority students: Where are we, and where do we need to go? *The Elementary School Journal* 96, 353–361.

Goodman, K.S. (1967) Reading: A psycholinguistic guessing game. *Journal of the Reading Specialist* 4, 126 –135.

Goodman, K.S. (1996) *On Reading*. Portsmouth, NH: Heinemann.

Goodman, Y., Watson, D. and Burke, C. (1987) *Reading Miscue Inventory: Alternative Procedures*. New York, NY: Owens.

Graves, D. (1983) *Writing: Teachers and Children at Work*. Portsmouth NH: Heinemann.

Greenleaf, C., Schoenbach, R., Cziko, C. and Mueller, F. (2001) Apprenticing adolescent readers to academic literacy. *Harvard Educational Review* 71, 79–125.

Gunning, T.G. (2000) *Creating Literacy Instruction for All Children* (3rd edn). Boston, MA: Allyn and Bacon.

Harris, T.L. and Hodges, R.E. (eds) (1995) *The Literacy Dictionary: The Vocabulary of Reading and Writing*. Newark, DE: International Reading Association.

Henderson, A.T. (1987) *The Evidence Continues to Grow: Parents Involvement Improves Student Achievement*. Columbus, MD: National Committee for Citizens in Education.

Henderson, A.T. and Berla, N. (1995) *A New Generation of Evidence: The Family is Critical to Student Achievement*. Washington, DC: The Center for Law and Education.

Holdaway, D. (1979) *Foundations of Literacy*. New York: Ashton Scholastic.

Hoover-Dempsey, K.V. and Sandler, H.M. (1995) Parental involvement in children's education. Why does it make a difference? *Teachers College Record* 97, 310–331.

Hornberger, N. (1989) Continua of biliteracy. *Review of Educational Research* 59, 271–296.

Hudelson, S. (1994) Literacy development of second language children. In F. Genesee (ed.) *Educating Second Language Children* (pp. 129–158). Cambridge: Cambridge University Press.

International Reading Association (1988) *New Directions in Reading Instruction*. Newark, DE: International Reading Association.

Jiménez, R.T. (1992) Opportunities and obstacles in bilingual reading. Unpublished doctoral dissertation, University of Illinois at Urbana-Champaign.

Jimenez, R.T. (1997) The facilitating effects of transfer on the reading comprehension of bilingual Latino/a students. In C.K. Kinzer, K.A. Hinchman and D.J. Leu (eds) *Inquiries in Literacy Theory and Practice: Forty-sixth Yearbook of the National Reading Conference* (pp. 147–155). Chicago: National Reading Conference.

Jiménez, R.T., Garcia, G.E. and Pearson, P.D. (1995) Three children, two languages, and strategic reading: Case studies in bilingual/monolingual reading. *American Educational Research Journal* 32, 67–97.

Jiménez, R.T., Garcia, G.E. and Pearson, P.D. (1996) The reading strategies of Latino/a students who are successful English readers: Opportunities and obstacles. *Reading Research Quarterly* 31 (1), 90–112.

Jimenez, R. and Gersten, R. (1999) Lessons and dilemmas derived from the literacy instruction of two Latina/o teachers. *American Educational Research Journal* 36, 265–301.

Krashen, S. (1981) *Second Language Acquisition*. Oxford: Pergamon.

Krashen, S. (1982) *Principles and Practices in Second Language Acquisition*. Oxford: Pergamon.

Krashen, S. (1999) *Condemned Without a Trial: Bogus Arguments Against Bilingual Education*. Portsmouth, NH: Heinemann

Kucer, S.B. (1986) Helping writers get the 'big picture.' *Journal of Reading* 30, 18–24.

Kucer, S.B. (1995) Guiding bilingual students 'through' the literacy processes. *Language Arts* 72, 20–29.

Kucer, S.B. (2001) *Dimensions of Literacy: A Conceptual Base for Teaching Reading and Writing in School Settings.* Mahwah, NJ: Erlbaum.

Kucer, S.B. and Silva, C. (in progress) *Teaching the Dimensions of Literacy.*

Kucer, S.B., Silva, C. and Delgado-Larocco, E. (1995) *Curricular Conversations: Themes in Multilingual and Monolingual Classrooms.* York, ME: Stenhouse.

Lau vs. Nichols (1974) 414 US. 563

Lerner, J.W. (2003) *Learning Disabilities: Theories, Diagnosis, and Teaching Strategies* (9th edn). New York: Houghton Mifflin.

Long, M.H. (1981) Input, interaction, and second language acquisition. In H. Winitz (ed.) *Native Language and Foreign Acquisition.* Annals of the New York Academy of Sciences, 379.

Mace-Matluck, B., Hoover, W. and Calfee, R. (1989) Teaching reading to bilingual children: A longitudinal study of teaching and learning in the early grades. *NABE Journal* 13, 187–216.

MacLachlan, P. (1985) *Sarah, Plain and Tall.* New York: Harper & Row.

Mohr, N. (1979) *Felita.* New York: Dial Press.

Moll, L. and Greenberg, J. (1990) Creating zones of possibilities: Combining social contexts for instruction. In L. Moll (ed.) *Vygotsky and Education: Instructional Implications and Applications of Sociohistorical Psychology* (pp. 319–348). Cambridge: Cambridge University Press.

Moore, C.C. (1985) A visit from St Nicholas, or 'Twas the night before Christmas.' In D. Hall (ed.) *The Oxford Book of Children's Verse in America.* New York, Oxford University Press

NCTM (1989) *Curriculum and Evaluation Standards for School Mathematics.* Reston, VA: National Council of Teachers of Mathematics.

Nelson, J. (1990) *Magic Money Machine.* New York: Modern Curriculum Press.

Neufeld, P. and Fitzgerald, J. (2001) Early English reading development: Latino English learners in the 'low' reading group. *Research in the Teaching of English* 36, 64–109.

New York State Education Department (1998) *English Language Arts: Resource Guide.* New York: New York State Education Department.

Nitko, A.J. (2001) *Educational Assessment of Students.* Upper Saddle River, NJ: Merrill Prentice-Hall.

Ogle, D.M. (1986) A teaching model that develops active reading of expositiory text. *The Reading Teacher* 39, 564–570.

Oller, J.W. and Perkins, K. (1980) *Research in Language Testing.* Rowley, MA: Newbury House.

O'Malley, J.M. and Valdez Pierce, L. (1996) *Authentic Assessment for English Language Learners.* Reading, MA: Addison Wesley.

Padron, Y. (1994) Comparing reading instruction in Hispanic/limited English-proficient schools and other inner-city schools. *Bilingual Research Journal* 18, 49–66.

Pappamihiel, N.E. (2002) English as a second language students and English language anxiety: Issues in the mainstream classroom. *Research in the Teaching of English* 36, 327–355.

Pearson, P.D. and Johnson, D.D. (1978) *Teaching Reading Comprehension.* New York: Holt, Rinehart, and Winston.

Peregoy, S. and Boyle, O. (1997) *Reading, Writing, and Learning in ESL: A Resource Book for K–12 Teachers.* New York: Longman.

Ramirez, J.D., Yuen, S.D. and Ramey, D.R. (1991) *Executive Summary: Final Report: Longitudinal Study of Structured English Immersion Strategy, Early-exit, and Late-exit Transitional Bilingual Educational Programs for Language Minority Children.* San Mateo, CA: Aquirre International.

Raphael, T.E. (1986) Teaching question/answer relationships, revisited. *Reading Teacher* 39, 516–522.

Rigg, P. and Allen, V. (eds) (1989) *When They Don't All Speak English: Integrating the ESL Student into the Regular Classroom.* Urbana, IL: NCTE.

Resnick, L.B. and Klopfer, L.E. (1989) Toward the thinking curriculum: An overview. In L.B. Resnick and L.E. Klopfer (eds) *Toward the Thinking Curriculum: Current Cognitive Research.* (pp. 1–18). Alexandria, VA: Association for Supervision and Curriculum.

Rhodes, L.K. and Dudley-Marling, C. (1988) *Readers and Writers with a Difference.* Portsmouth, NH: Heinemann.

Rosenblatt, L.M. (1978) *The Reader, The Text, The Poem.* Carbondale, IL: Southern Illinois University Press.

Rosenblatt, L. (1991) Literature: S.O.S.! *Language Arts* 68, 444–448.

Ruddell, R.B. (2002) *Teaching Children to Read and Write: Becoming an Effective Literacy Teacher* (3rd edn). Boston, MA: Allyn and Bacon.

Ruddell, R., Ruddell, M. and Singer, H. (1994) *Theoretical Models and Processes of Reading* (4th edn). Newark, DE: IRA.

Rumelhardt, D.E. (1980) Schemata: The building blocks of cognition. In R. J. Spiro, B.C. Bruce and W.F. Brewer (eds) *Theoretical Issues in Reading Comprehension* (pp. 33–58). Hillsdale, NJ: Erlbaum.

Salomon, J. and Rhodes, N.C. (1995) *Conceptualizing Academic Language.* Santa Cruz, CA: National Center for Research on Cultural Diversity and Second Language Learning.

Schiffini, A. (1996) Reading instruction for the pre-literate and struggling older student. *NABE News* 6, 20, 30.

Schmidt, P.R. (1993) Literacy development of two bilingual, ethnic-minority children in a kindergarten program. In D.J. Leu and C.K. Kinzer (eds) *Examining Central Issues in Literacy Research, Theory, and Practice: Forty-Second Yearbook of the National Reading Conference* (pp. 189–196). Chicago, IL: National Reading Conference.

Schoenbach, R., Greenleaf, C., Cziko, C. and Hurwitz, L. (1999) *Reading for Understanding: A Guide to Improving Reading in Middle and High School Classroom.* San Francisco, CA: Jossey-Bass.

Shartrand, A. Weiss, H. Kreider, H. and Lopez, M. (1997) *New Skills for New Schools: Preparing Teachers in Family Involvement.* Cambridge, MA: Harvard Family Research Project, Harvard Graduate School of Education.

Silva, C. and Delgado-Larocco, E. (1993) Facilitating learning through interconnections: A conceptual approach to core literature units. *Language Arts* 70, 469–474.

Smith, F. (1971) *Understanding Reading: A Psycholinguistic Analysis of Reading and Learning to Read.* New York: Holt, Rinehart.

Spiro, R.J., Vispoel, W., Schmitz, W., Samarapungavan, A. and Boerger, A. (1987) Knowledge acquisition for application: Cognitive flexibility and transfer in complex content domains. In B.C. Britton and S. Glynn (eds) *Executive Control Functions in Reading.* Hillsdale, NJ: Erlbaum.

Stiggins, R.J. (1988) Revitalizing classroom assessment: The highest instructional priority. *Phi Delta Kappan* 69, pp. 363–368.

Terrell, T.D. (1981) The natural approach in bilingual education. In California State Department of Education, *Schooling and Language Minority Students: A Theoretical Framework* (pp. 117–146). Los Angeles: Evaluation, Dissemination and Assessment Center, California State University.

Thomas, W. and Collier, V. (1996) *Language Minority Students Achievement and Program Effectiveness.* Fairfax, VA: Center for Bilingual/Multicultural/ESL Education.

Thomas, W. and Collier, V. (1997) *School Effectiveness for Language Minority Students.* Washington, DC: National Clearinghouse for Bilingual Education.

Tierney, R. and Pearson, P.D. (1994) Learning from text: A framework for improving classroom practice. In R. Ruddell, M. Ruddell and H. Singer (eds) *Theoretical Models and Processes of Reading* (4th edn; pp. 496–513). Newark, DE: International Reading Association.

Tompkins, G.E. (1998) *50 Literacy Strategies: Step by Step.* Upper Saddle River, NJ: Merrill-Prentice Hall.

Tompkins, G.E. (2001) *Literacy for the 21st Century: A Balanced Approach* (2nd edn). Upper Saddle River, NJ: Merrill-Prentice Hall.

US Department of Education (1997) *A Profile of Policies and Practices for Limited English Proficient Students: Screening Methods, Program Support, and Teacher Training* (SASS 1993–94; NCES 97–472). Washington, DC: Government Printing Office.

US Department of Education (2001) *No Child Left Behind* (PL107–110). Washington, DC: Government Printing Office.

Vacca, R.T. and Vacca, J.L. (1986) *Content Area Reading*. Boston: Little Brown.

Verhoeven, L.T. (1994) Transfer in bilingual development: The linguistic interdependence hypothesis revisited. *Language Learning* 44, 381–415.

Vygotsky, L.S. (1962) *Thought and Language*. Cambridge, MA: MIT.

Vygotsky, L.S. (1978) In M. Cole, V. John Steiner, S. Scribner and E. Souberman (eds) *Mind in Society*. Cambridge, MA: Harvard University.

Wells, G. (1986) *The Meaning Makers*. Portsmouth, NH: Heinemann.

Wertsch, J. (ed.) (1985) *Culture, Communication, and Cognition*. London: Cambridge University Press.

Index

Subjects